Benvenuto!

Just Enough **Italian**

D. L. Ellis, C. Mariella

Pronunciation **Dr. J. Baldwin**

PASSPORT BOOKS
NTC/Contemporary Publishing Group

The publishers would like to thank the Italian State Tourist
Office (ENIT) for their help in the preparation of this book.

This edition first published in 1983 by Passport Books,
a division of NTC/Contemporary Publishing Group, Inc.,
4255 West Touhy Avenue,
Lincolnwood (Chicago), Illinois 60712-1975 U.S.A.
Manufactured in the United States of America.
International Standard Book Number: 0-8442-9503-5

1 2 3 4 5 6 7 8 9 QP 19

Contents

Using the phrase book

● This phrase book is designed to help you get by in Italy, to get what you want or need. It concentrates on the simplest but most effective way you can express these needs in an unfamiliar language.

● The CONTENTS on p. 5 give you a good idea of which section to consult for the phrase you need.

● The INDEX on p. 153 gives you more detailed information about where to look for your phrase.

● When you have found the right page you will be given:
  either – the exact phrase
  or   – help in making up a suitable sentence
  and   – help in getting the pronunciation right

● The English sentences in **bold** type will be useful for you in a variety of different situations, so they are worth learning by heart. (See also DO IT YOURSELF, p. 143.)

● Wherever possible you will find help in understanding what Italian people say to *you* in reply to your questions.

● If you want to practise the basic nuts and bolts of the language further, look at the DO IT YOURSELF section starting on p. 143.

● Note especially these three sections:
  Everyday expressions p. 11
  Shop talk p. 57
  Public notices p. 123
  You are sure to want to refer to them most frequently.

● When you arrive in Italy make good use of the tourist information offices (see p. 24).
  North American addresses:

Italian National Travel Office
500 North Michigan Avenue
Suite 1046
Chicago, IL 60611
(312) 644-0990

Italian National Travel Office
360 Post Street
Suite 801
San Francisco, CA 94108
(415) 392-6206

Italian National Travel Office
630 Fifth Avenue
New York, NY 10111
(212) 245-4822

Italian National Travel Office
3 Place Ville Marie
Montreal, Canada
H3B2E3
(514) 866-7667

A note on the pronunciation system

In traveler's phrase books there is usually a pronunciation section which tries to teach English-speaking tourists how to correctly pronounce the language of the country they are visiting. This is based on the belief that in order to be understood, the speaker must have an accurate, authentic accent—that he must pronounce every last word letter-perfectly.

The authors of this book, on the other hand, wanted to devise a workable and usable pronunciation system. So they had to face the fact it is absolutely impossible for an average speaker of English who nas no technical training in phonetics and phonetic transcription systems (which includes 98% of all the users of this book!) to reproduce the sounds of a foreign language with perfect accuracy, just from reading a phonetic transcription, cold—no prior background in the language. We also believe that you don't have to have perfect pronunciation in order to make yourself understood in a foreign country. After all, natives you run into will take into account that you are foreigners, and visitors, and more than likely they will feel gratified by your efforts to communicate and will probably go out of their way to try to understand you. They may even help you, and correct you, in a friendly manner. We have found, also, that visitors to a foreign country are not usually concerned with perfect pronunciation—they just want to get their message across, to communicate!

With this in mind, we have designed a pronunciation system which is of the utmost simplicity to use. This system does not attempt to give an accurate—but also problematical and tedious—representation of the sound system of the language, but instead uses common sound and letter combinations in English which are the closest to the sounds in the foreign language. In this way, the sentences transcribed for pronunciation should be read as naturally as possible, as if they were ordinary English. In no way does the user have to attempt to make the words sound "foreign." So, while to yourselves you will sound as if you are speaking ordinary English—or at least making ordinary English sounds—you will at the same time be making yourselves understood in another language. And, as the saying goes, practice makes perfect, so it is probably a good idea to repeat aloud to yourselves several times the phrases you think you are going to use, before you actually use them. This will give you greater confidence, and will also help in making yourself understood.

In Italian it is important to stress, or emphasize the syllables in *italics*, just as you would if we were to take as an English example: L*i*ttle Jack H*o*rner s*a*t in the c*o*rner. Here we have ten syllables but only four stresses. This Italian sentence also has ten syllables but only four stresses: qu*e*sta m*a*cchina è rumor*o*sa (this car is noisy).

Of course you may enjoy trying to pronounce a foreign language as well as possible and the present system is a good way to start. However, since it uses only the sounds of English, you will very soon need to depart from it as you imitate the sounds you hear the native speaker produce and begin to relate them to the spelling of the other language. Italian will pose no problems as there is an obvious and consistent relationship between pronunciation and spelling.

Divertitevi!

Regions and regional capitals

Everyday expressions

[See also 'Shop talk', p. 57.]

Hello ⌉	**Buon giorno**
	boo-*on* jorno
Good morning ⌉	Ciao (friends only)
Good day (before lunch) ⌋	chow
Good afternoon (after lunch)⌉	**Buona sera**
Good evening ⌋	boo-*ona* seh-ra
Good night	**Buona notte**
	boo-*ona* not-teh
Good-bye	**A rivederci**
	ah reeveh-d*e*irchee
See you later	**A piú tardi**
	ah pew tardee
Yes	**Sí**
	see
Please	**Per favore**
	pair fav-*oreh*
Yes, please	**Sí grazie**
	see gratzee-eh
Great!	**Magnifico!**
	man-*yeefeeco*
Thank you	**Grazie**
	gratzee-eh
Thank you very much	**Molte grazie**
	molteh gratzee-eh
That's right	**Esatto**
	ez*at*-to
No	**No**
	noh
No thank you	**No, grazie**
	noh gratzee-eh
I disagree	**Non sono d'accordo**
	non sonno dak-kordo
Excuse me ⌉	**Scusi**
Sorry ⌋	sc*oozee*
Don't mention it ⌉	**Prego**
That's OK ⌋	preg-o

That's good ⎤	**Va bene**
I like it ⎦	va ben-eh
That's no good ⎤	**Non va bene**
I don't like it ⎦	non va ben-eh
I know	**Lo so**
	lo so
I don't know	**Non lo so**
	non lo so
It doesn't matter	**Non importa**
	non importa
Where's the toilet, please?	**Dov'è il bagno, per favore?**
	dov-eh il ban-yo pair fav-oreh
How much is that? [*point*]	**Quanto costa?**
	quanto costa
Is the service included?	**Il servizio è compreso?**
	il sairvitzio eh compraizo
Do you speak English?	**Parla inglese?**
	parla inglaizeh
I'm sorry ...	**Mi dispiace ..**
	mee dispi-ah-cheh ...
I don't speak Italian	**non parlo italiano**
	non parlo italian-o
I only speak a little Italian	**parlo solo un poco italiano**
	parlo solo oon poco italian-o
I don't understand	**non capisco**
	non capisco
Please can you ...	**Per favore potrebbe ...**
	pair fav-oreh potreb-beh ...
repeat that?	**ripetere?**
	ripet-ereh
speak more slowly?	**parlare piú lentamente?**
	parlar-eh pew lentamenteh
write it down?	**scriverlo?**
	screeverlo
What is this called in Italian? [*point*]	**Come si dice questo in italiano?**
	com-eh see deecheh questo in italian-o

Crossing the border

ESSENTIAL INFORMATION

- Don't waste time just before you leave rehearsing what you're going to say to the border officials – the chances are that you won't have to say anything at all, especially if you travel by air.
- It's more useful to check that you have your documents handy for the journey: passport, tickets, money, travellers' cheques, insurance documents, driving licence and car registration documents.
- Look out for these signs:

  ALT! (stop!)
  CONTROLLO PASSAPORTI (passport control)
  DOGANA (customs)
  POLIZIA DI FRONTIERA (border police)
  FRONTIERA (border)

  [*For further signs and notices see p. 123.*]
- You may be asked routine questions by the customs officials [*see below*]. If you have to give personal details see 'Meeting people', p. 14. The other important answer to know is 'Nothing':

  Niente (nee-*enteh*).

ROUTINE QUESTIONS

Passport?	**Passaporto?**
	pas-sap*orto*
Insurance?	**Assicurazione?**
	as-sicooratz*ioneh*
Registration document?	**Libretto di circolazione?**
(logbook)	libret-to dee cheercolatzi-*oneh*
Ticket, please	**Biglietto, prego**
	bil-*yet*-to pr*eg*-o
Have you anything to declare?	**Ha niente da dichiarare?**
	ah nee-*enteh* da dikee-ar*ar*-eh
Where are you going?	**Dove va?**
	d*ov*-eh va
How long are you staying?	**Per quanto tempo rimane?**
	pair qu*anto* t*empo* reem*an*-eh
Where have you come from?	**Da dove viene?**
	da d*ov*-eh vee-*ehneh*

You may also have to fill in forms which ask for:

surname	**cognome**
first name	**nome**
date of birth	**data di nascita**
place of birth	**luogo di nascita**
address	**indirizzo**
nationality	**nazionalità**
profession	**professione**
passport number	**numero passaporto**
issued at	**emesso a**
signature	**firma**

Meeting people

[*See also* 'Everyday expressions', *p. 11.*]

Breaking the ice

Hello ⎤
Good morning ⎦
How are you?

Buon giorno (Ciao)
boo-*on* jorno (chow)
Come sta? (Come stai?)
com-eh st*a* (com-eh st*a*-ee)

(Expressions above in parenthesis should only be used with people you know well.)

Pleased to meet you	**Piacere**
	pee-ach*ai*reh
I am here . . .	**Sono qui . . .**
	sonno qu*ee* . . .
on holiday	**in vacanza**
	in vac-*an*tza
on business	**per affari**
	pair aff*ar*-ee
Can I offer you . . .	**Posso offrirle . . .**
	pos-so offr*eer*-leh . . .
a drink?	**da bere?**
	da b*ai*reh
a cigarette?	**una sigaretta?**
	oona sigar*et*-ta

a cigar?	**un sigaro?**
	oon *see*garo
Are you staying long?	**Rimane per molto?**
	reem*an*-eh pair *molto*

Name

What's your name?	**Come si chiama?**
	com-eh see kee-*am*-**ah**
My name is ...	**Mi chiamo ...**
	mee kee-*am*-o ...

Family

Are you married?	**Lei è sposato/a***
	lay eh spoz*at*-o/-**ah**
I am ...	**Sono ...**
	sonno ...
married	**sposato/a***
	spoz*at*-o/-ah
single	**da sposare**
	da spoz*ar*-eh
This is ...	**Le presento ...**
	leh pre*sento* ...
my wife	**mia moglie**
	mee-ah m*o*l-yeh
my husband	**mio marito**
	mee-o mar*ee*to
my son	**mio figlio**
	mee-o f*ee*l-yo
my daughter	**mia figlia**
	mee-ah f*ee*l-ya
my (boy) friend	**il mio ragazzo**
	il mee-o rag*at*-tzo
my (girl) friend	**la mia ragazza**
	la mee-ah rag*at*-tza
my (male) colleague	**il mio collega**
	il mee-o col-*leg*-ah
my (female) colleague	**la mia collega**
	la mee-ah col-*leg*-ah

* For men use 'o', for women use 'a'.

Do you have any children?	Lei ha bambini?
	lay ah bambeenee
I have ...	Ho ...
	o ...
one daughter	una figlia
	oona feel-ya
one son	un figlio
	oon feel-yo
two daughters	due figlie
	dooeh feel-yeh
three sons	tre figli
	treh feel-yee
No, I haven't any children	No, non ho bambini
	noh non o bambeenee

Where you live

Are you ...	Lei è ...
	lay eh ...
Italian?	italiano/a?*
	italian-o/-ah
Swiss?	svizzero/a?*
	svit-tzero/ah
I am ...	Sono ...
	sonno ...
American	americano/a*
	american-o/-ah
English	inglese
	inglatzeh

[For other nationalities, see p. 136]

I live ...	Abito ...
	ah-beeto ...
in London	a Londra
	ah londra
in England	in Inghilterra
	in ing-ill-tairra

[For other countries see p. 136.]

* For men use 'o', for women use 'a'.

in the north	al nord
	al nord
in the south	al sud
	al sood
in the east	all'est
	al-laist
in the west	all'ovest
	al-lovaist
in the centre	al centro
	al chentro

For the businessman and woman

I'm from ... (firm's name)	Sono della ...
	sonno del-la ...
I have an appointment with...	Ho un appuntamento con ...
	o oon ap-poontamento con ...
May I speak to ... ?	Potrei parlare con ... ?
	potray parlar-eh con ...
This is my card	Ecco il mio biglietto da visita
	ec-co il mee-o bil-yet-to da vizita
I'm sorry, I'm late	Mi dispiace, sono in ritardo
	mee dispi-ah-cheh sonno in reetardo
Can I fix another appointment?	Potrei fissare un altro appuntamento?
	potray fis-sar-eh oon altro ap-poontamento
I'm staying at the (Paris) Hotel	Sono all'hotel (Parigi)
	sonno al-lotel (par-eejee)
I'm staying in (St John's) Road	Sto in via (San Giovanni)
	sto in vee-ah (san jovan-nee)

Asking the way

ESSENTIAL INFORMATION

● Keep a look-out for all these place names as you will find them on shops, maps and notices.

WHAT TO SAY

Excuse me, please
Scusi, per favore
sc*oo*zee, pair fav-*oreh*

How do I get ...
Per andare ...
pair and*a*r-eh ...

to Rome?
a Roma?
ah roma

to the Via Nomentana?
in via Nomentana?
in vee-ah noment*an*-ah

to the Hotel Torino?
all'hotel Torino?
al-lot-*e*l tor*ee*no

to the airport?
all'aeroporto?
al-la-airop*o*rto

to the beach?
alla spiaggia?
al-la spee-*a*d-ja

to the bus station?
alla stazione degli autobus?
al-la statzi*o*neh del-yee ah-*oo*tobus

to the historic site?
al centro storico?
al ch*e*ntro st*o*rico

to the market?
al mercato?
al mairc*a*t-o

to the police station?
alla stazione di polizia?
al-la statzi*o*neh dee politz*ee*-ah

to the port?
al porto?
al p*o*rto

to the post office?
all'ufficio postale?
al-loof-f*ee*cho post*a*l-eh

to the railway station?
alla stazione ferroviaria?
al-la statzi*o*neh ferrovee-*ar-ee-ah*

to the sports stadium?
allo stadio?
al-lo st*a*d-eeo

to the tourist information office?	all'ufficio informazioni turistiche?
	al-loof-*feecho* informatzion*ee* toor*i*stikeh
to the town centre?	in centro?
	in ch*e*ntro
to the town hall?	al Municipio?
	al moonich*ee*-peeo
Excuse me, please	Scusi, per favore
	sc*oo*zee pair fav-*oreh*
Is there . . . nearby?	C'è . . . qui vicino?
	cheh . . . quee veech*ee*no
an art gallery	una galleria d'arte
	*oo*na gal-ler*ee*-ah d*a*rteh
a baker's	una panetteria
	*oo*na panet-ter*ee*-ah
a bank	una banca
	*oo*na b*a*nca
a bar	un bar
	*oo*n bar
a botanical garden	un giardino botanico
	*oo*n jard*ee*no bot*a*n-eeco
a bus stop	una fermata d'autobus
	*oo*na fairm*a*t-ah d*a-oo*tobus
a butcher's	una macelleria
	*oo*na machel-ler*ee*-ah
a café	un caffè
	*oo*n caf-*feh*
a cake shop	una pasticceria
	*oo*na pasteet-chair*ee*-ah
a campsite	un campeggio
	*oo*n camp*e*d-jo
a car park	un parcheggio
	*oo*n park*e*d-jo
a change bureau	un ufficio del cambio
	*oo*n oof-*feecho* del c*a*mbeeo
a chemist's	una farmacia
	*oo*na farmach*ee*-ah
a church	una chiesa
	*oo*na kee-*e*hza
a cinema	un cinema
	*oo*n ch*ee*nema

Is there . . . nearby?	C'è . . qui vicino?
	cheh . . . quee veech*eeno*
a delicatessen	una salumeria
	oona saloomer*ee*-ah
a dentist's	un dentista
	oon dent*ee*sta
a department store	un grande magazzino
	oon gr*a*ndeh magad-dz*eeno*
a disco	una discoteca
	oona discot*ec*-ah
a doctor's surgery	uno studio medico
	oono st*oo*dio m*e*d-eeco
a dry-cleaner's	una lavanderia a secco
	oona lavander*ee*-ah ah s*ec*-co
a fishmonger's	una pescheria
	oona pesker*ee*-ah
a garage (for repairs)	un' autoriparazioni
	oon a-ootoriparatzi-*onee*
a hairdresser's	un parrucchiere
	oon par-rooc-kee-*ai*reh
a greengrocer's	un verduriere
	oon vairdoo-ree-*ai*reh
a grocer's	un alimentari
	oon alimen-t*a*r-ee
a hardware shop	un negozio di ferramenta
	oon neg*o*tzio dee ferram*e*nta
a Health and Social Security Office	una sezione dell'INAM
	oona setzioneh del-l*ee*nam
a hospital	un ospedale
	oon osped*a*l-eh
a hotel	un hotel
	oon otel
an ice-cream parlour	una gelateria
	oona jelat-er*ee*-ah
a laundry	una lavanderia
	oona lavander*ee*-ah
a museum	un museo
	oon mooz*e*h-o
a newsagent's	un'edicola
	oonedeecola

a night club	**un night**
	oon night
a petrol station	**un distributore**
	oon distribootoreh
a post box	**una buca per lettere**
	oona booca pair let-tereh
a public garden (town park)	**un giardino pubblico**
	oon jardeeno poob-blico
a public toilet	**un gabinetto pubblico**
	oon gabinet-to poob-blico
a restaurant	**un ristorante**
	oon ristoranteh
a (snack) bar	**un bar**
	oon bar
a sports ground	**un campo sportivo**
	oon campo sporteevo
a supermarket	**un supermercato**
	oon sooper-maircat-o
a sweet shop	**una pasticceria**
	oona pasteet-chairee-ah
a swimming pool	**una piscina**
	oona pisheena
a taxi stand	**una stazione taxi**
	oona statzioneh taxi
a telephone	**un telefono**
	oon telephono
a theatre	**un teatro**
	oon teh-atro
a tobacconist's	**un tabaccaio**
	oon tabac-cah-yo
a travel agent's	**un'agenzia di viaggi**
	oonajentzee-ah dee vee-ad-jee
a youth hostel	**un ostello per la gioventú**
	oon ostel-lo pair la joventoo
a zoo	**uno zoo**
	oono.dzor

DIRECTIONS

- Asking where a place is, or if a place is nearby, is one thing; making sense of the answer is another.
- Here are some of the most important key directions and replies.

Left	**Sinistra** sin*ee*stra
Right	**Destra** d*e*stra
Straight on	**Sempre diritto** s*e*mpreh deer*ee*t-to
There	**Là** la
First left/right	**La prima a sinistra/destra** la pr*e*ema ah sin*ee*stra/d*e*stra
Second left/right	**La seconda a sinistra/destra** la sec*o*nda ah sin*ee*stra/d*e*stra
At the crossroads	**All'incrocio** alleencr*o*-cho
At the traffic lights	**Al semaforo** al sem*a*phoro
At the roundabout	**Alla rotonda** al-la rot*o*nda
At the level crossing	**Al passaggio a livello** al pas-s*a*d-jo ah leev*e*l-lo
It's near/far	**È vicino/lontano** eh veech*ee*no/lont*a*n-o
One kilometre	**Un chilometro** oon keel*o*metro
Two kilometres	**Due chilometri** d*oo*eh keel*o*metree
Five minutes . . .	**Cinque minuti . . .** ch*i*nqueh min*oo*tee .
on foot	**a piedi** ah pee-*e*hdee
by car	**in macchina** in m*a*c-keena

Take ...	Prenda ...
	prenda ...
the bus	l'autobus
	la-*oo*tobus
the train	il treno
	il tren-o
the tram	il tram
	il tram
the underground	la metropolitana
	la metro-poleet*a*n-ah

[*For public transport see p. 114.*]

The tourist information office

ESSENTIAL INFORMATION

- Most towns and even villages in Italy have a tourist information office, run by the regional or local tourist boards.
- Look for these words:
  UFFICIO INFORMAZIONI TURISTICHE
  ENTE TURISMO
- You can also get information from the Touring Club and Automobile Club offices, often indicated with the abbreviations TCI (Italian Touring Club) and ACI (Italian Automobile Club). ACI also offers help with car repairs or accidents.
- These offices give you free information in the form of printed leaflets, fold-outs, brochures, lists and plans.
- You may have to pay for some types of document, but this is not usual.
- For finding a tourist office, see p. 18.

WHAT TO SAY

Please have you got . . .
Per favore avete . .
pair fav-*oreh* avet-eh . . .

a plan of the town?
una piantina della città?
oona pee-ant*eena* del-la cnit-*ca*

a list of hotels?
un elenco degli alberghi?
oon elen-co del-yee alb*air*-ghee

a list of campsites?
un elenco dei campeggi?
oon elen-co day camped-jee

a list of restaurants?
un elenco dei ristoranti?
oon elen-co day ristor*antee*

a list of coach excursions?
un elenco di gite in autobus?
oon elen-co dee jeeteh in
ah-*oo*toboos

a list of events?
un elenco di avvenimenti?
oon elen-co dee av-venim*entee*

a leaflet on the town?
un opuscolo sulla città?
oon op*oos*-colo sool-la chit-*ta*

a leaflet on the region?
un opuscolo sulla regione?
oon op*oos*-colo sool-la reh-jon*eh*

a railway timetable?	un orario ferroviario?
	oon or-*a*reeo ferrovi-*ar*-eeo
a bus timetable?	un orario degli autobus?
	oon or*ar*-eeo d*e*l-yee ah-*oo*toboos
In English, please	In inglese, per favore
	in ingl*ai*zeh pair fav-*o*reh
How much do I owe you?	Quanto Le devo?
	qu*a*nto leh d*e*v-o
Can you recommend ...	Mi potrebbe raccomandare ...
	mee potr*e*b-beh rac-comand*a*r-eh...
a cheap hotel?	un albergo non caro?
	oon alb*ai*r-go non c*a*r-o
a cheap restaurant?	un ristorante non caro?
	oon ristor*a*nte non c*a*r-o
Can you make a booking for me?	Potrebbe prenotare per me?
	potr*e*b-beh prenot-*a*r-eh pair m*e*h

LIKELY ANSWERS

You need to understand when the answer is 'No'. You should be able to tell by the assistant's facial expression, tone of voice and gesture, but there are some language clues, such as:

No	No
	noh
I'm sorry	Mi dispiace
	mee dispi-*a*h-cheh
I don't have a list of campsites	Non ho un elenco dei campeggi
	non o oon el*e*n-co day camped-jee
I haven't got any left	Non ne ho piú
	non neh o p*e*w
It's free	È gratis
	eh gr*a*t-is

Hotel

ESSENTIAL INFORMATION

- If you want hotel-type accommodation, all the following words in capital letters are worth looking for on name boards:
  HOTEL $\big\}$ (hotel)
  ALBERGO
  MOTEL (two main chains are run by **ACI** and **Agip**)
  PENSIONE (boarding house)
- Hotels are divided into five classes (from luxury to tourist class) and **pensioni** into three.
- Lists of hotels and **pensioni** can be obtained from local tourist offices or the Italian National Travel Office [*see p. 24*].
- The cost is displayed in the room itself, so you can check it when having a look round before agreeing to stay.
- The displayed cost is for the room itself, per night and not per person. Breakfast is extra and therefore optional.
- Service and VAT are always included in the cost of the room, so tipping is voluntary.
- Not all hotels provide meals, apart from breakfast. **A pensione** always provides meals. Breakfast is continental-style: coffee or tea, with rolls and jam.
- An identity document is requested when registering at a hotel and will normally be kept overnight. Passports or driving licences are accepted.
- Finding a hotel, see p. 18.

WHAT TO SAY

I have a booking	**Ho una prenotazione**
	o oona prenotatzi-*o*neh
Have you any vacancies, please?	**Avete delle camere libere, per favore?**
	avet-eh del-leh *c*amereh *l*ee*b*ereh pair fav-*o*reh

Can I book a room?	**Potrei prenotare una camera?**
	potr*ay* prenot-*ar*-eh *oo*na camera
It's for ...	**È per ...**
	eh pair ...
one person	**una persona**
	*oo*na pairsona
two people	**due persone**
	d*oo*eh pairsoneh

[For numbers see p.128.]

It's for ...	**È per ...**
	eh pair ...
one night	**una notte**
	*oo*na not-teh
two nights	**due notti**
	d*oo*eh not-tee
one week	**una settimana**
	*oo*na set-timan-**ah**
two weeks	**due settimane**
	d*oo*eh set-timan-eh
I would like ...	**Vorrei ...**
	vorr*ay* ...
a room	**una camera**
	*oo*na camera
two rooms	**due camere**
	d*oo*eh camereh
with a single bed	**singola/e ***
	s*i*ngola/eh
with two single beds	**a due letti**
	ah d*oo*eh let-tee
with a double bed	**con un letto matrimoniale**
	con oon let-to matrimon-*yal*-eh
with a toilet ⎤ with a bathroom ⎦	**con bagno**
	con b*an*-yo
with a shower	**con doccia**
	con d*ot*-cha
with a cot	**con una culla**
	con *oo*na c*oo*l-la
with a balcony	**con terrazza**
	con terr*at*-tza

* Use 'a' for one single bed, 'e' for two single beds.

I would like ...
Vorrei ...
vorr*ay* ...

full board
pensione completa
pen-see*o*neh compl*e*t-ah

half board
mezza pensione
med-dza pen-see*o*neh

bed and breakfast
solo colazione
[see Essential information]
solo colatzioneh

Do you serve meals?
Servite i pasti?
sairv*ee*teh ee p*a*stee

At what time is ...
A che ora è ...
ah keh ora *e*h ...

breakfast?
la colazione?
la colatzioneh

lunch?
il pranzo?
il pr*a*ntzo

dinner?
la cena?
la ch*e*n-ah

How much is it?
Quanto costa?
qu*a*nto c*o*sta

Can I look at the room?
Potrei vedere la stanza?
potr*ay* ved-*ai*reh la st*a*ntza

I'd prefer a room ...
Preferirei una stanza ...
prefairee-*ray* oona st*a*ntza ...

at the front/at the back
sul davanti/sul retro
sool dav*a*ntee/sool r*e*tro

I'd like a quiet room
Vorrei una camera tranquilla
vorr*ay* *o*ona c*a*mera tranqu*ee*l-la

OK, I'll take it
Va bene, la prendo
va b*e*n-eh la pr*e*ndo

No thanks, I won't take it
No grazie, non la prendo
noh gr*a*tzee-eh non la pr*e*ndo

The key to number (10), please
Per favore la chiave del numero (dieci)
pair fav-*o*reh la kee-*a*hveh del n*oo*mero (dee-*e*chee)

Please may I have ...
Per favore, potrei avere ...
pair fav-*o*reh potr*ay* av*ai*reh ..

a coat hanger?
un attaccapanni?
oon at-tac-cap*a*n-nee

a towel?	**un asciugamano?**
	oon ashoogarnan-o
a glass?	**un bicchiere?**
	oon beec-kee-*ai*reh
some soap?	**del sapone?**
	del sap*o*neh
an ashtray?	**un portacenere?**
	oon portach*ai*nereh
another pillow?	**un altro cuscino?**
	oon altro coosh*ee*no
another blanket?	**un'altra coperta?**
	oon*a*ltra cop*ai*rta
Come in!	**Avanti!**
	av*a*ntee
One moment, please!	**Un momento, per favore!**
	oon momento pair fav-*o*reh
Please can you ...	**Per favore, potrebbe ...**
	pair fav-*o*reh potr*e*b-beh ...
do this laundry/dry-cleaning?	**far lavare questo/far lavare questo a secco?**
	far lav*a*r-eh qu*e*sto/far lav*a*r-eh qu*e*sto ah s*e*c-co
call me at ...?	**chiamarmi alle ...?**
	kee-am*a*rmee al-leh ...
help me with my luggage?	**aiutarmi con i bagagli?**
	ah-yoot*a*rmee con ee bag*a*l-yee
call be a taxi for ...?	**chiamarmi un taxi per le ...?**
	kee-am*a*rmee oon t*a*xi pair leh ...
[*For times see p. 130.*]	
The bill, please	**Il conto, per favore**
	il c*o*nto pair fav-*o*reh
Is service included?	**Il servizio è compreso?**
	il sairv*i*tzio eh compr*ai*zo
I think this is wrong	**Penso che questo sia sbagliato**
	penso keh qu*e*sto see-ah sbal-y*a*t-o
May I have a receipt?	**Potrei avere una ricevuta?**
	potr*ay* av*ai*reh oona reechev*oo*ta

At breakfast

Some more ... please	**Ancora ... per favore** ancora ... pair fav-*oreh*
coffee	**del caffè** del caf-*feh*
tea	**del tè** del *teh*
bread	**del pane** del *pan*-eh
butter	**del burro** del *boorro*
jam	**della marmellata** del-la marmel-*lat*-ah
May I have a boiled egg?	**Potrei avere un uovo à la coque?** potr*ay* av*aireh* oon *wov*-o ah la coc

LIKELY REACTIONS

Have you an identity
    document, please?
	Ha un documento di
	    riconoscimento, per favore?
	ah oon doc*oo*mento dee
	    riconosheemento pair fav-*oreh*

What's your name? [see p. 15]	**Come si chiama?** com-eh see kee-*am*-ah
Sorry, we're full	**Spiacente, siamo al completo** spee-a*chenteh* see-*am*-o al complet-o
I haven't any rooms left	**Non ci sono piú camere** non chee sonno pew *camereh*
Do you want to have a look?	**Vuole vederla?** voo-*oleh* ved-*air*la
How many people is it for?	**Per quante persone?** pair qu*anteh* pairsoneh
From (seven o'clock) onwards	**Dalle (sette) in poi** dal-leh (set-teh) in poy
From (midday) onwards	**Da (mezzogiorno) in poi** da (med-dzojorno) in poy
[For times see p. 130.]	
It's (10,000) lira	**Fa (diecimila) lire** fa (dee-echee meela) leereh
[For numbers see p. 128.]	

Camping and youth hostelling

ESSENTIAL INFORMATION

Camping

● Look for the words: **CAMPING** or **CAMPEGGIO** or this sign.

● Be prepared to have to pay:
  per person
  for the car (if applicable)
  for the tent or caravan plot
  for electricity
  for hot showers
● You must provide proof of identity, such as your passport.
● You can obtain lists of campsites from local tourist offices [*see p. 24*] and from the Italian National Travel Office.
● To book plots in advance (particularly recommended in July and August) write to the **Centro Internazionale Prenotazioni Campeggio, Casella Postale 649, 1-50100 Firenze, Italy.**
● Some campsites offer discounts to campers with the International Camping Carnet.
● Camping off-site is allowed except in state forests and national parks. It is always best to ask permission from the landowner.

Youth hostels

- Look for the words:
  OSTELLO PER LA
  GIOVENTÙ, or this sign.
- You will be asked for a
  YHA card and your
  passport on arrival.
- Food and cooking facilities
  vary from hostel to hostel
  and you may have to help
  with domestic chores.
- You will have to hire sheets on arrival.
- In the high season it is advisable to book beds in advance, and your stay will be limited to a maximum of three consecutive nights per hostel.
- Apply to ENIT or local tourist offices in Italy [see p. 24] for lists of youth hostels and details of regulations for hostellers.
- For buying or replacing camping equipment, see p. 54.

WHAT TO SAY

I have a booking	Ho una prenotazione
	o oona prenotatzi-oneh
Have you any vacancies?	Avete dei posti liberi?
	avet-eh day postee leeberee
It's for ...	È per ...
	eh pair ...
one adult/one person	un adulto/una persona
	oon adoolto/oona pairsona
two adults/two people	due adulti/due persone
	dooeh adooltee/dooeh pairsoneh
and one child	e un bambino
	eh oon bambeeno
and two children	e due bambini
	eh dooeh bambeenee
It's for ...	È per ...
	eh pair ...
one night	una notte
	oona not-teh

two nights	due notti
	dooeh not-tee
one week	una settimana
	oona set-timan-ah
two weeks	due settimane
	dooeh set-timan-eh
How much is it ...	Quant'è ...
	quanteh ...
for the tent?	per la tenda?
	pair la tenda
for the caravan?	per la roulotte?
	pair la roolot
for the car?	per la macchina?
	pair la mac-keena
for the electricity?	per l'elettricità?
	pair lelet-treechita
per person?	per persona?
	pair pairsona
per day/night?	per giorno/notte?
	pair jorno/not-teh
May I look round?	Potrei dare uno sguardo?
	potray dar-eh oono zgoo-ardo
At what time do you lock up at night?	A che ora chiudete di sera?
	ah keh ora kee-oodet-eh dee seh-ra
Do you provide anything ...	È possibile ...
	eh posseebeeleh ...
to eat?	mangiare qui?
	manjar-eh quee
to drink?	bere qui?
	baireh quee
Do you have ...	Avete ...
	avet-eh ...
a bar?	un bar?
	oon bar
hot showers?	docce con acqua calda?
	dot-cheh con acqua calda
a kitchen?	una cucina?
	oona coocheena
a laundry?	una lavanderia?
	oona lavanderee-ah
a restaurant?	un ristorante?
	oon ristoranteh

Do you have . . .   **Avete . . .**
                                av*et*-eh . . .

  a shop?   **un negozio?**
                                 oon neg*o*tzi-**o**

  a swimming pool?   **una piscina?**
                                 oona pish*ee*na

[For food shopping see p. 61, and for eating and drinking out see p. 81.]

Where are . . .   **Dove sono . . .**
                                 d*o*v-eh s*o*nno . . .

  the dustbins?   **le pattumiere?**
                                 leh pat-toomee-*aireh*

  the showers?   **le docce?**
                                 leh d*o*t-cheh

  the toilets?   **i gabinetti?**
                                 ee gabin*et*-tee

At what time must one . . .   **A che ora si deve . . .**
                                 ah keh *o*ra see d*e*v-eh . . .

  go to bed?   **andare a dormire?**
                                 and*a*r-eh ah dorm*ee*reh

  get up?   **alzare?**
                                 alt*za*r-eh

Please have you got . . .   **Per favore avete . . .**
                                 pair fav-*o*reh av*et*-eh . . .

  a broom?   **una scopa?**
                                 oona sc*o*p-ah

  a corkscrew?   **un cavatappi?**
                                 oon cavat*a*p-pee

  a drying-up cloth?   **uno straccio per asciugare?**
                                 o*o*no str*a*t-cho pair ashoog*a*r-eh

  a fork?   **una forchetta?**
                                 oona fork*et*-ta

  a fridge?   **un frigorifero?**
                                 oon frigor*ee*efero

  a frying pan?   **una padella per friggere?**
                                 oona pad*e*l-la pair fr*ee*d-**jereh**

  an iron?   **un ferro da stiro?**
                                 oon f*e*rro da st*ee*ro

  a knife?   **un coltello?**
                                 oon colt*e*l-lo

  a plate?   **un piatto?**
                                 oon pee-*at*-to

a saucepan?	una pentola? oona pentola
a teaspoon?	un cucchiaino? oon cooc-kee-ah-*eeno*
a tin opener?	un apriscatole? oon apreescat-oleh
any washing powder?	della polvere per lavare? del-la polvereh pair lavar-**eh**
any washing-up liquid?	del liquido per lavare i piatti? del liquido pair lavar-eh ee pee-*at*-tee
The bill, please	Il conto, per favore il conto pair fav-*oreh*

Problems

The toilet	Il gabinetto il gabinet-to
The shower	La doccia la dot-cha
The tap	Il rubinetto il roobinet-to
The razor point	La spina per il rasoio la speena pair il razoyo
The light	La luce la loocheh
... is not working	... non funziona ... non foontzi-ona
My camping gas has run out	La bombola del gas è finita la bombola del gaz eh feeneeta

LIKELY REACTIONS

Have you an identity document?	Ha un documento di riconoscimento? ah oon docoomento dee riconosheemento
Your membership card, please	La sua tessera, per favore la soo-ah tes-saira pair fav-*oreh*
What's your name? [see p. 15]	Come si chiama? com-eh see kee-*am*-ah
Sorry, we're full	Spiacente, siamo al completo spee-achenteh see-*am*-o al complet-o

How many people is it for?	**Per quante persone?**
	pair qu*a*nteh pairs*o*neh
How many nights is it for?	**Per quante notti?**
	pair qu*a*nteh n*o*t-tee
It's (8,000) lira ...	**Fa (ottomila) lire ...**
	fa (*o*t-tom*è*ela) l*ee*reh ...
per day/per night	**al giorno/per notte**
	al j*o*rno/pair n*o*t-teh

[*For numbers see p. 128.*]

Rented accommodation: problem solving

ESSENTIAL INFORMATION

- If you are looking for accommodation to rent, look out for:
  DA AFFITTARE/AFFITTANSI (for rent)
  APPARTAMENTO/ALLOGGIO (apartment)
  VILLA (villa)
  VILLETTA/VILLINO (cottage)
  CHALET (chalet)
- For arranging details of your rental, see 'Hotel' p. 26.
- Key words you will meet if renting on the spot:
  il deposito   deposit
  il dep*o*z-eeto
  le chiavi   keys
  leh kee-*a*hvee
- Having arranged your own accommodation and arrived with the key, check the obvious basics that you take for granted at home.
  Electricity: Voltage? Razors and small appliances brought from home may need adjusting. You may need an adaptor.
  Gas: Town gas or bottled gas? Butane gas must be kept indoors, propane gas must be kept outdoors.
  Stove: Don't be surprised to find:
  the grill inside the oven, or no grill at all
  a lid covering the rings which lifts up to form a 'splashback'
  a mixture of two gas rings and two electric rings
  Toilet: Mains drainage or septic tank? Don't flush disposable diapers or anything else down the toilet if you are on a septic tank.
  Water: Find the stopcock. Check taps and plugs—they may not

operate in the way you are used to. Check how to turn on (or light) the hot water.

Windows: Check the method of opening and closing windows and shutters.

Insects: Is an insecticide spray provided? If not, get one locally.

Equipment: See p. 54 for buying or replacing equipment.

● You will probably have an official agent, but be clear in your own mind who to contact in an emergency, even if it is only a neighbour in the first place.

WHAT TO SAY

My name is ...	Mi chiamo ...
	mee kee-*am*-o ...
I'm staying at ...	Sono al ...
	sonno al ...
They've cut off ...	Hanno interrotto ...
	*a*n-no interr*o*t-to ...
the electricity	l'elettricità
	lelet-treechi*ta*
the gas	il gas
	il gaz
the water	l'acqua
	l*a*cqua
Is there ... in the area?	C'è .. nella zona?
	cheh ... nel-la d*zo*na
an electrician	un elettricista
	oon elet-treech*i*sta
a plumber	un idraulico
	oon idr*a*-oolico
a gas fitter	un addetto al gas
	oon ad-d*e*t-to al gaz
Where is ...	Dov'è ...
	dov-*eh* ...
the fuse box?	la scatola dei fusibili?
	la sc*a*t-ola day foo*zee*bilee
the stopcock?	il rubinetto principale?
	il roobin*e*t-to princheep*a*l-eh
the boiler?	il bruciatore del riscaldamento?
	il broo-cha-t*o*reh del riscaldam*e*nto
the water heater?	lo scalda-acqua?
	lo scalda-*a*cqua

Is there . . .	C'è . . .
	cheh . . .
town gas?	il gas di città?
	il gaz dee chit-*ta*
bottled gas?	gas in bombola?
	gaz in bombola
a septic tank?	una fossa settica?
	oona *fos*-sa *set*-teeca
central heating?	il riscaldamento centrale?
	il riscaldam*en*to chentr*al*-eh
The cooker	Il fornello
	il forn*el*-lo
The hair dryer	L'asciugacapelli
	lashoogacap*el*-lee
The heating	Il riscaldamento
	il riscaldam*en*to
The immersion heater	Il boiler
	il *boi*lair
The iron	Il ferro da stiro
	il *fe*rro da st*ee*ro
The pilot light	La fiammella spia
	la fee-am-m*el*-la sp*ee*-ah
The refrigerator	Il frigorifero
	il frigor*ee*fero
The telephone	Il telefono
	il tel*e*phono
The toilet	Il gabinetto
	il gabin*et*-to
The washing machine	La lavatrice
	la lavatr*ee*cheh
The water heater	Lo scalda-acqua
	lo scalda-*ac*qua
. . . is not working	. . . non funziona
	. . . non foontzi-*ona*
Where can I get . . .	Dove posso trovare . . .
	dov-eh *pos*-so trov*ar*-eh . . .
an adaptor for this?	una spina per questo?
	oona sp*ee*na pair qu*es*to
a bottle of butane gas?	una bombola di gas butano?
	oona b*o*mbola dee gaz boot*an*-o
a bottle of propane gas?	una bombola di gas propano?
	oona b*o*mbola dee gaz prop*an*-o

a fuse?	**un fusibile?**
	oon foozeebeeleh
an insecticide spray?	**una bombola insetticida?**
	oona bombola inset-ticheeda
a light bulb?	**una lampadina?**
	oona lampadeena
The drain	**Lo scarico**
	lo scarico
The sink	**Il lavandino**
	il lavandeeno
The toilet	**Il gabinetto**
	il gabinet-to
... is blocked	**... è otturato**
	... eh ot-toorat-o
The gas is leaking	**Il gas perde**
	il gaz pairdeh
Can you mend it straightaway?	**Può ripararlo subito?**
	poo-oh riparar-lo soobeeto
When can you mend it?	**Quando potrà ripararlo?**
	quando potra riparar-lo
How much do I owe you?	**Quanto Le devo?**
	quanto leh dev-oh
When is the rubbish collected?	**Quando raccolgono i rifiuti?**
	quando rac-colgono ee ree-fewtee

LIKELY REACTIONS

What's your name?	**Come si chiama?**
	com-eh see kee-am-ah
What's your address?	**Il suo indirizzo?**
	il soo-o indeerit-tzo
There's a shop ...	**C'è un negozio ...**
	cheh oon negotzi-o ...
in town	**in città**
	in chit-ta
in the village	**in paese**
	in pa-aiz-eh
I can't come ...	**Non posso venire ...**
	non pos-so veneereh ...
today	**oggi**
	od-jee

this week	questa settimana
	questa set-timan-ah
until Monday	fino a lunedì
	feeno ah loon-edee
I can come ...	Posso venire ...
	pos-so veneereh ...
on Tuesday	martedì
	mart-edee
when you want	quando vuole
	quando voo-oleh
Every day	Ogni giorno
	on-yee jorno
Every other day	Un giorno sí e uno no
	oon jorno see eh oono noh
On Wednesdays	Tutti i mercoledí
	toot-tee ee maircol-edee

[*For days of the week see p. 132.*]

General shopping

The drug store/The chemist's

ESSENTIAL INFORMATION

- Look for the word **FARMACIA** (drug store) or this sign.
- Medicines (drugs) are only available at a drug store.
- Some non-drugs can be bought at a supermarket or department store.
- Try the drug store *before* going to a doctor: they are usually qualified to treat minor injuries.
- Drug stores take it in turns to stay open all night and on Sundays. A notice on the door headed **FARMACIE DI TURNO** or **SERVIZIO NOTTURNO** gives details of opening times.
- Some toiletries can also be bought at a **PROFUMERIA**, but they will be more expensive.
- Finding a pharmacist, see p. 18.

WHAT TO SAY

I'd like . . .	Vorrei . . .
	vorr*ay* . . .
some Alka Seltzer	dell'Alka Seltzer
	del-l*alka* s*eltzer*
some antiseptic	dell'antisettico
	del-l*antiset-tico*
some aspirin	dell'aspirina
	del-l*aspireena*
some bandage	delle bende
	del-l*eh* b*endeh*
some cotton wool	del cotone
	del cot*oneh*
some eye drops	del collirio
	del col-l*ee-reeo*

I'd like . . .	Vorrei . . .
	vorr*ay* . . .
some foot powder	del talco per piedi
	del t*a*lco pair pee-*eh*dee
some gauze dressing	della ga*r*za
	del-la g*a*rdza
some inhalant	dell'inalante
	del-linal*a*nteh
some insect repellent	della crema anti-insetti
	del-la crem-ah anti-ins*et*-tee
some lip salve	della crema per le labbra
	del-la cr*e*m-ah pair leh l*a*b-bra
some nose drops	delle gocce per il naso
	del-leh g*o*t-cheh pair il n*a*z-o
some sticking plaster	del cerotto
	del ch*ai*rot-to
some throat pastilles	delle pastiglie per la gola
	del-leh past*eel*-yeh pair la g*o*la
some Vaseline	della Vaselina
	del-la vazel*ee*na
I'd like something for . . .	Vorrei qualcosa per . . .
	vorr*ay* qualc*o*za pair . . .
bites	morsicature
	mor-seecat*oo*reh
burns	bruciature
	broo-chat*oo*reh
chilblains	screpolature
	screp-olat*oo*reh
a cold	il raffreddore
	il raf-fred-d*o*reh
constipation	stitichezza
	stitik*et*-tza
a cough	la tosse
	la t*o*s-seh
diarrhoea	diarrea
	dee-arr*eh*-ah
ear-ache	mal d'orecchie
	mal dor*r*ek-kee-*eh*
flu	influenza
	influ*e*ntza
scalds	scottature
	scot-tat*oo*reh

sore gums	**mal di gengive**
	mal dee jen*jeeveh*
sprains	**distorsioni**
	distor-see*onee*
stings	**punture**
	poon*tooreh*
sunburn	**scottature da sole**
	scot-ta*tooreh* da *sol*-eh
car (sea/air) sickness	**mal d'auto (di mare/d'aereo)**
	mal d*a*-ooto (dee m*areh*/da-*eh*-reho)
I need ...	**Avrei bisogno di ...**
	avr*ay* beez*on*-yo **dee ...**
some baby food	**cibi per bambini**
	cheebee pair bamb*eenee*
some contraceptives	**contraccettivi**
	contrat-chet-*teevee*
some deodorant	**deodorante**
	deh-odor*anteh*
some disposable nappies	**pannolini per bambini**
	pan-nol*eenee* pair bamb*eenee*
some hand cream	**crema per le mani**
	crem-ah pair leh m*an*-ee
some lipstick	**un rossetto**
	oon ros-s*et*-to
some make-up remover	**latte detergente**
	lat-teh deterg*enteh*
some paper tissues	**fazzoletti di carta**
	fat-tzol*et*-tee dee c*arta*
some razor blades	**lamette per rasoio**
	lam*et*-teh pair raz*oy*o
some safety pins	**spille di sicurezza**
	sp*eel*-leh dee sicoor*et*-tza
some sanitary towels	**assorbenti igienici**
	as-sorb*enti* eej*en-eechi*
some shaving cream	**crema da barba**
	crem-ah da b*arba*
some soap	**sapone**
	sap*oneh*
some sun-tan lotion/oil	**crema/olio solare**
	crem-ah/*oly*o sol*ar-eh*
some talcum powder	**borotalco**
	borot*alco*

I need ...	Avrei bisogno di ...
	avray beezon-yo dee ...
some Tampax	**Tampax**
	tampax
some toilet paper	**carta igienica**
	carta eejen-eeca
some toothpaste	**dentifricio**
	denteefreecho

[For other essential expressions see 'Shop talk', p. 57.]

Holiday items

ESSENTIAL INFORMATION

● Places to shop at and signs to look for:

LIBRERIA-CARTOLERIA	(stationery)
TABACCHERIA	(smoke shop)
ARTICOLI DA REGALO	(presents)
FOTO-OTTICO	(photographer – optician)
ARTICOLI FOTOGRAFICI	(photographical items)

● and the main department stores:
UPIM
STANDA
RINASCENTE

WHAT TO SAY

Where can I buy ... ?	**Dove posso comprare ... ?**
	dov-eh pos-so comprar-eh ...
I'd like ...	**Vorrei ...**
	vorray ...
a bag	**una borsa**
	oona borsa
a beach ball	**un pallone da spiaggia**
	oon pal-loneh da speead-ja
a bucket	**un secchiello**
	oon sec-kee-ello

an English newspaper	**un giornale inglese**
	oon jorn*a*l-eh ingl*ai*zeh
some envelopes	**delle buste**
	del-leh b*oo*steh
a guide book	**una guida**
	oona gw*ee*da
a map (of the area)	**una piantina (della zona)**
	oona pee-ant*ee*na (del-la dz*o*na)
some postcards	**delle cartoline**
	del-leh cartol*ee*neh
a spade	**una paletta**
	oona pal*e*t-ta
a straw hat	**un cappello di paglia**
	oon cap-p*e*l-lo dee p*a*l-ya
a suitcase	**una valigia**
	oona val*ee*-ja
some sunglasses	**degli occhiali da sole**
	del-yee oc-kee-*a*l-ee da s*o*leh
a sunshade	**un parasole**
	oon paras*o*leh
an umbrella	**un ombrello**
	oon ombr*e*l-lo
some writing paper	**della carta da lettere**
	del-la c*a*rta da l*e*t-tereh
I'd like . . . [*show the camera*]	**Vorrei . . .**
	vorr*ay* . . .
a colour film	**una pellicola a colori**
	oona pel-l*ee*cola ah col*o*ree
a black and white film	**una pellicola in bianco e nero**
	oona pel-l*ee*cola in bee-*a*nco eh
	n*ai*ro
for prints	**per fotografie**
	pair fotograf*ee*-eh
for slides	**per diapositive**
	pair dee-apozeet*ee*veh
12 (24/36) exposures	**da dodici (ventiquattro/trentasei)**
	pose
	da dod*ee*chee (venteecoo-*a*t-tro/
	trentas*ay*) p*o*zeh
a standard 8 mm film	**un film da otto millimetri normale**
	oon feelm da *o*t-to meel-l*ee*metree
	norm*a*l-eh

I'd like . . . [*show the camera*]	**Vorrei . . .**
	vorr*ay* . .
a super 8 film	**un film super otto**
	oon feelm s*oo*per *o*t-to
some flash bulbs	**delle lampadine per flash**
	del-leh lampad*ee*neh pair flash
This camera is broken	**Questa macchina fotografica è rotta**
	questa m*a*c-keena fotogr*a*feeca eh r*o*t-ta
The film is stuck	**Il film è bloccato**
	il feelm eh bloc-c*a*t-o
Please can you . . .	**Per favore potrebbe . . .**
	pair fav-*o*reh potr*e*b-beh . . .
develop/print this?	**sviluppare/stampare questo?**
	zveeloop-p*a*r-eh/stamp*a*r-eh questo
load the camera?	**caricare il film?**
	ca-ree-c*a*r-eh il feelm

[*For other essential expressions see 'Shop talk', p. 57.*]

The smoke shop

**ESSENTIAL
INFORMATION**

- Tobacco is sold where you see this sign.
- See p. 18 to ask if there is one nearby.
- Smoke shops always sell postage stamps and salt.
- A smoke shop is sometimes part of a café-bar, a stationery (**CARTOLERIA**) or newsstand.

WHAT TO SAY

A packet of cigarettes ...	**Un pacchetto di sigarette ...** oon pac-*ket*-to dee sigar*et*-teh ...
with filters	**con filtro** con *fee*ltro
without filters	**senza filtro** sentza *fee*ltro
king size	**formato lungo** form*a*t-o l*oo*ngo
menthol	**al mentolo** al ment*o*lo
Those up there ...	**Quelle là sopra ...** qu*e*l-leh la s*o*pra ...
on the right	**a destra** ah d*e*stra
on the left	**a sinistra** ah sin*ee*stra

These [*point*]	**Queste** questeh
Cigarettes, please	**Sigarette, per favore** sigaret-teh pair fav-oreh
100, 200, 300, two packets	**Cento, duecento, trecento, due pacchetti** chento dooeh-chento treh-chento dooeh pac-ket-tee
Have you got ...	**Avete ...** avet-eh ...
English cigarettes?	**sigarette inglesi?** sigaret-teh inglaizee
American cigarettes?	**sigarette americane?** sigaret-teh american-eh
English pipe tobacco?	**tabacco inglese da pipa?** tabac-co inglaizeh da peepa
American pipe tobacco?	**tabacco americano da pipa?** tabac-co american-o da peepa
rolling tobacco?	**tabacco sciolto?** tabac-co sholto
A packet of pipe tobacco	**Un pacchetto di tabacco da pipa** oon pac-ket-to dee tabac-co da peepa
That one up there ...	**Quello là sopra ...** quel-lo la sopra ...
on the right	**a destra** ah destra
on the left	**a sinistra** ah sineestra
This one [*point*]	**Questo** questo
A cigar, please	**Un sigaro, per favore** oon seegaro pair fav-oreh
This one [*point*]	**Questo** questo
Some cigars	**Dei sigari** day seegaree
Those [*point*]	**Quelli** quel-lee
A box of matches	**Una scatola di cerini** oona scat-ola dee chereenee

A packet of pipe cleaners	**Un pacchetto di filtri per pipa** oon pac-ket-to dee filtree pair peepa
[*show lighter*] A packet of flints	**Un pacchetto di pietrine** oon pac-ket-to dee pee-etreeneh
Lighter fuel	**Della benzina per accendino** del-la bendzeena pair at-chendeeno
Lighter gas, please	**Gas per accendino, per favore** gaz pair at-chendeeno pair fav-oreh

[*For other essential expressions see 'Shop talk', p. 57.*]

Buying clothes

ESSENTIAL INFORMATION

- Look for:
  ABBIGLIAMENTO PER SIGNORA (women's clothes)
  ABBIGLIAMENTO DA UOMO (men's clothes)
  CALZATURE (shoes)
- Don't buy without being measured first or without trying things on.
- Don't rely on conversion charts of clothing sizes [see p. 142].
- If you are buying for someone else, take their measurements with you.
- The department stores **STANDA, UPIM** and **RINASCENTE** all sell clothes and shoes.

WHAT TO SAY

I'd like ...	Vorrei ...
	vorray ...
an anorak	una giacca a vento
	oona jac-ca ah vento
a belt	una cintura
	oona chintoora
a bikini	un due pezzi
	oon dooeh pet-tzee
a bra	un reggiseno
	oon red-jee-sehno
a cap (swimming)	una cuffia (da bagno)
	oona coof-fee-ah (da ban-yo)
a cap (skiing)	un berretto (da sci)
	oon berret-to (da shee)
a cardigan	un golf
	oon golf
a coat	un cappotto
	oon cap-pot-to
a dress	un vestito
	oon vesteeto
a hat	un cappello
	oon cap-pel-lo

a jacket	una giacca
	oona jac-ca
a jumper	una maglia
	oona mal-ya
a nightdress	una camicia da notte
	oona cameecha da not-teh
a pair of pyjamas	un pigiama
	oon pid-jam-ah
a V-neck pullover	un pullover
	oon pool-lovair
a raincoat	un impermeabile
	oon impermeh-ah-beeleh
a shirt	una camicia
	oona cameecha
a skirt	una gonna
	oona gon-na
a suit	un completo
	oon complet-o
a swimming costume	un costume da bagno
	oon costoomeh da banyo
a T-shirt	una maglietta di cotone
	oona mal-yet-ta dee cotoneh
I'd like a pair of ...	Vorrei un paio di ...
	vorray oon payo dee ...
briefs (women)	mutandine
	mootandeeneh
gloves	guanti
	gwantee
jeans	jeans
	jeens
shorts	pantaloni corti
	pantalon-ee cortee
socks (short/long)	calze (corte/lunghe)
	caltzeh (corteh/loong-geh)
stockings	calze di nylon
	caltzeh dee nylon
tights	collants
	col-lan
trousers	pantaloni
	pantalon-ee
underpants (men)	slip da uomo
	slip da womo

I'd like a pair of ...	**Vorrei un paio di ...**
	vor*ray* oon *p*ayo dee ...
shoes	**scarpe**
	sc*a*rpeh
canvas shoes	**scarpe di tela**
	sc*a*rpeh dee *t*eh-la
sandals	**sandali**
	s*a*ndalee
beach shoes	**sandali da spiaggia**
	s*a*ndalee da spee-*a*d-ja
smart shoes	**scarpe eleganti**
	sc*a*rpeh eleg*a*ntee
boots	**stivali**
	stee-v*a*l-ee
moccasins	**mocassini**
	mocas-s*ee*nee
My size is ...	**Porto il numero ...**
[*For numbers see p. 128.*]	porto il n*oo*mero ...
Can you measure me, please?	**Può prendermi la misura, per favore?**
	poo-*o* prendermi la meez*oo*ra pair fav-*o*reh
Can I try it on?	**Posso provare?**
	p*o*s-so provar-*e*h
It's for a present	**È per un regalo**
	eh pair oon regal-*o*
These are the measurements ...	**Queste sono le misure ...**
[*show written*]	qu*e*steh s*o*nno leh miz*oo*reh ...
bust	**petto**
	p*e*t-to
chest	**torace**
	tor*a*cheh
collar	**colletto**
	col-*le*t-to
hip	**fianchi**
	fee-*a*nkee
leg	**gamba**
	g*a*mba
waist	**vita**
	v*e*eta

Have you got something . . .	Avete qualcosa . . .
	avet-eh qualcoza . . .
in black?	in nero?
	in nairo
in white?	in bianco?
	in bee-anco
in grey?	in grigio?
	in greed-jo
in blue?	in blu?
	in bloo
in brown?	in marrone?
	in marroneh
in pink?	in rosa?
	in roza
in green?	in verde?
	in vairdeh
in red?	in rosso?
	in ros-so
in yellow?	in giallo?
	in jal-lo
in this colour? [point]	in questo colore?
	in questo coloreh
in cotton?	in cotone?
	in cotoneh
in denim?	in jeans?
	in jeens
in leather?	in pelle?
	in pel-leh
in nylon?	in nylon?
	in nylon
in suede?	in pelle scamosciata?
	in pel-leh scamoshat-ah
in wool?	in lana?
	in lan-ah
in this material? [point]	in questo tessuto?
	in questo tes-sooto

[*For other essential expressions see 'Shop talk', p. 57.*]

Replacing equipment

ESSENTIAL INFORMATION

- Look for these shops and signs:

ELETTRICISTA	(electrical goods)
FERRAMENTA	
ELETTRODOMESTICI	(hardware)
ARTICOLI PER LA CASA	
DROGHERIA	(household cleaning materials)

- In a supermarket look for this display:
  ARTICOLI CASALINGHI
- To ask the way to the shop see p. 18.
- At a campsite try their shop first.

WHAT TO SAY

Have you got ...	Avete ...
	avet-eh ...
an adaptor? [*show appliance*]	una spina a riduzione?
	oona speena ab ridootzioneh
a bottle of butane gas?	una bombola di gas butano?
	oona bombola dee gaz bootan-o
a bottle of propane gas?	una bombola di gas propano?
	oona bombola dee gaz propan-o
a bottle opener?	un apribottiglie?
	oon ap-reebot-teel-yeh
a corkscrew?	un cavatappi?
	oon cavat-tap-pee
any disinfectant?	del disinfettante?
	del disinfet-tanteh
any disposable cups?	dei bicchieri da buttare?
	day beec-kee-airee da boot-tar-eh
any disposable plates?	dei piatti da buttare?
	day pee-at-tee da boot-tar-eh
a drying-up cloth?	uno straccio per asciugare?
	oono strat-cho pair ashoogar-eh
any forks?	delle forchette?
	del-leh forket-teh

a fuse? [*show old one*]	un fusibile?
	oon fooz*eebeeleh*
an insecticide spray?	uno spray insetticida?
	oono spr*a-ee* inset-teech*eeda*
a paper kitchen roll?	un rotolo di carta da cucina?
	oon rotolo dee c*arta* da cooch*eena*
any knives?	dei coltelli?
	day coltel-lee
a light bulb? [*show old one*]	una lampadina?
	oona lampad*eena*
a plastic bucket?	un secchio in plastica?
	oon sec-keeo in pl*asteeca*
a plastic can?	un recipiente di plastica?
	oon recheepee-*enteh* dee pl*astceca*
a scouring pad?	una paglietta abrasiva?
	oona pal-*yet*-ta abras*eeva*
a spanner?	una chiave inglese?
	oona kee-*ah*veh ingl*aizeh*
a sponge?	una spugna?
	oona spoon-ya
any string?	del cordino?
	del cord*eeno*
any tent pegs?	dei picchetti da tenda?
	day pic-ket-tee da t*enda*
a tin opener?	un apriscatole?
	oon apreesc*at*-oleh
a torch?	una torcia?
	oona torcha
any torch batteries?	delle pile?
	del-leh p*eeleh*
a universal plug (for the sink)?	un tappo (per lavandino)?
	oon t*ap*-po (pair lavand*eeno*)
a washing line?	una corda per stendere?
	oona corda pair stend*ereh*
any washing powder?	della polvere da lavare?
	del-la polvereh da lav*ar*-eh
a washing-up brush?	uno spazzolino per piatti?
	oono spat-tzol*eeno* pair pee-*at*-tee
any washing-up liquid?	del sapone liquido per piatti?
	del sap*oneh* l*iquido* pair pee-*at*-tee

[*For other essential expressions see 'Shop talk', p. 57.*]

Shop talk

ESSENTIAL INFORMATION

- Know your coins and bills:
  coins: see illustration
  bills: L500, L1000, L2000, L5000, L10,000, L20,000, L50,000
- Know how to say the important weights and measures:

50 grams	**cinquanta grammi**
	chinquanta gram-mee
100 grams	**cento grammi**
	chento gram-mee
200 grams	**duecento grammi**
	dooeh-chento gram-mee
½ kilo	**mezzo chilo**
	med-dzo keelo
1 kilo	**un chilo**
	oon keelo
2 kilos	**due chili**
	dooeh keelee
½ litre	**mezzo litro**
	med-dzo leetro
1 litre	**un litro**
	oon leetro
2 litres	**due litri**
[*For numbers see p. 128.*]	dooeh leetree

- You may see the words **etto** (100 grams) or **all'etto** (per 100 grams) on price tickets. This is a colloquial expression for 100 grams.
- In small shops don't be surprised if customers, as well as the shop assistant, say 'hello' and 'good-bye' to you.

CUSTOMER

Hello ⎤	**Buon giorno**
Good morning ⎦	boo-*on* jorno
Good afternoon (after 3 p.m.)	**Buona sera**
	boo-*ona* seh-ra
Good-bye	**A rivederla**
	ah reeveh-*dairla*
I'm just looking	**Guardo soltanto**
	gwardo soltanto

Excuse me	**Mi scusi**
	mee sc*oo*zee
How much is this/that?	**Quanto costa questo/quello?**
	qu*a*nto c*o*sta qu*e*sto/qwel-**lo**
What's that?	**Che cos' è quello?**
	keh coz-*e*h quel-lo
What are those?	**Che cosa sono quelli?**
	keh c*o*za s*o*nno quel-**lee**
Is there a discount?	**C'è uno sconto?**
	cheh *oo*no sc*o*nto
I'd like that, please	**Vorrei quello, per favore**
	vorr*a*y quel-lo pair fav-*o*reh
Not that	**Non quello**
	non qu*e*l-lo
Like that	**Come quello**
	com-eh qu*e*l-lo
That's enough, thank **you**	**Basta così grazie**
	b*a*sta c*o*zee gr*a*tzee-eh
More, please	**Ancora, per favore**
	anc*o*ra pair fav-*o*reh
Less than that	**Meno di così**
	men-o dee c*o*zee
That's fine] OK	**Va bene**
	va b*e*n-eh
I won't take it, thank you	**Non lo prendo, grazie**
	non lo pr*e*ndo gr*a*tzee-eh
It's not right	**Non va bene**
	non va b*e*n-eh
Thank you very much	**Molte grazie**
	m*o*lteh gr*a*tzee-eh
Have you got something ...	**Avete qualcosa ...**
	av*e*teh qualc*o*za ...
better?	**di meglio?**
	dee m*e*l-yo
cheaper?	**di meno caro?**
	dee m*e*n-o c*a*r-o
different?	**di diverso?**
	dee deev*ai*rso
larger?	**di piú grande?**
	dee pew gr*a*ndeh
smaller?	**di piú piccolo?**
	dee pew p*i*c-colo

At what time do you ...	A che ora ...
	ah keh ora ...
open?	aprite?
	apreeteh
close?	chiudete?
	kewdet-eh
Can I have a bag, please?	Posso avere una borsa, per favore?
	pos-so avaireh oona borsa pair fav-oreh
Can I have a receipt?	Posso avere la ricevuta?
	pos-so avaireh la reechevoota
Do you take ...	Accettate ...
	at-chet-tat-eh ...
English/American money?	soldi inglesi/americani?
	soldee inglaizee/american-ee
travellers' cheques?	travellers' cheques?
	travellairs sheck
credit cards?	carte di credito?
	carteh dee cred-eeto
I'd like ...	Vorrei ...
	vorray ...
one like that	uno di quelli
	oono dee quel-lee
two like that	due di quelli
	dooeh dee quel-lee

SHOP ASSISTANT

Can I help you?	È da servire?
	eh da sairveereh
What would you like?	Che cosa desidera?
	keh coza dezeedera
Will that be all?	È tutto?
	eh toot-to
Is that all?	Basta così?
	basta cozee
Anything else?	Nient'altro?
	nee-entaltro
Would you like it wrapped?	Glielo incarto?
	lee-el-o incarto

Sorry, none left	**Mi dispiace non ne ho più** mee dispi-*ah*-cheh non nen o pew
I haven't got any	**Non ne abbiamo** non neh ab-bee-*am*-o
I haven't got any more	**Non ne abbiamo più** non neh ab-bee-*am*-o pew
How many do you want?	**Quanti ne desidera?** qu*an*tee neh dez*ee*dera
How much do you want?	**Quanto ne vuole?** quanto neh vwoleh
Is that enough?	**È abbastanza?** eh ab-bast*an*tza

Shopping for food

Bread

ESSENTIAL INFORMATION

- Finding a baker's, see p. 18.
- Key words to look for:

  PANETTERIA (baker's)
  PANIFICIO (baker's bread usually baked on premises)
  PANETTIERE (baker)
  PANE (bread)

- Supermarkets of any size nearly always sell bread.
- Opening times vary slightly from place to place but are generally 9–1 and 3.30–8. Most bakers open earlier than other shops and are closed one day a week – the day varies from town to town.
- Although large and small loaves can be bought, rolls are very popular and it is important to note that bread is usually bought by *weight*.
- Bakers often stock other groceries, particularly milk. There is no milk delivery service and the dairy (LATTERIA) is fast disappearing.

WHAT TO SAY

Some bread, please	Del pane, per favore
	del *pan*-eh pair fav-*o*reh
A loaf (like that)	Una pagnotta (così)
	oona pan-*yot*-ta (co*zee*)
A large one	Una grande
	oona *grand*eh
A small one	Una piccola
	oona *pic*-cola
A bread roll	Un panino
	oon pan*ee*no
250 grams of ...	Duecentocinquanta grammi di ...
	dooeh-ch*ento*-chinqu*anta* gram-mee dee ...

½ kilo of ...	**Mezzo chilo di ...**
	med-dzo keelo dee ...
1 kilo of ...	**Un chilo di ...**
	oon keelo dee ...
bread	**pane**
	pan-eh
white bread	**pane bianco**
	pan-eh bee-anco
wholemeal bread	**pane integrale**
	pan-eh integral-eh
bread rolls	**panini**
	paneenee
crispy bread sticks	**grissini**
	gris-seenee
Two loaves	**Due pagnotte**
	dooeh pan-yot-teh
Four bread rolls	**Quattro panini**
	quat-tro paneenee

[*For other essential expressions see 'Shop talk', p. 57.*]

Cakes

ESSENTIAL INFORMATION

- Key words to look for:
PASTICCERIA	(cake shop)
PASTICCIERE	(pastry maker)
PASTE/DOLCI	(cakes, pastries, sweets)
- To find a cake shop, see p. 19.
- BAR-PASTICCERIA: a place to buy cakes and have a drink. Italians often go to a bar for a snack mid-morning as they eat very little for breakfast.
- Most bars only have a few tables and charge more for waiter service. See p. 81, 'Ordering a drink'.

WHAT TO SAY

The type of cakes in the shops varies from region to region, but it is usual to find a variety of biscuits and small cream-filled pastries called paste fresche. These are bought by weight and it is best to point to the selection you prefer.

100 grams of ...	**Cento grammi di ...**
	chento gram-mee dee ...
200 grams of ...	**Duecento grammi di ..**
	dooeh-chento gram-mee dee ...
$\frac{1}{2}$ kilo of ...	**Mezzo chilo di ...**
	med-dzo keelo dee ...
cream pastries	**paste fresche**
	pasteh freskeh
biscuits	**biscotti**
	biscot-tee
A selection, please	**Misto, per favore**
	meesto pair fav-oreh

You may want to buy larger pastries and cakes individually:

A cake (like that), please	**Una torta (così), per favore**
	oona tor-ta cozee pair fav-oreh
An (apple) tart	**Una crostata (di mele)**
	oona crostat-a dee mele
A doughnut	**Un bombolone**
	oon bomboloneh
A brioche	**Una brioche**
	oona bree-osh

[*For other essential expressions see 'Shop talk', p. 57.*]

Ice-cream and sweets

ESSENTIAL INFORMATION

- Key words to look for:
GELATI	(ice-creams)
GELATERIA ⎤ CREMERIA ⎦	(ice-cream parlour)
PASTICCERIA	(cake shop)
- If you see a sign with GELATI-PRODUZIONE PROPRIA, this means that the ice-creams are made daily on the premises and are particularly good.
- Best known ice-cream brand-names are:
ALEMAGNA	CHIAVACCI
ALGIDA	MOTTA
BESANA	SAMMONTANA
- Every gelateria and cremeria has its own specialities which will either be described on menu cards or displayed on posters. Specialities vary from region to region.
- Pre-packed sweets are also available in supermarkets, bars and bakers' shops.

WHAT TO SAY

A ... ice, please	Per favore, un gelato ... pair fav-oreh oon jelat-o ...
chocolate	al cioccolato al choc-colat-o
lemon	al limone al leemoneh
nougat	al torroncino al torroncheeno
peach	alla pesca al-la pesca
pistachio	al pistacchio al peestac-keeo
strawberry	alla fragola al-la fragola
vanilla	alla crema al-la crem-ah

(1,000) lira's worth	**Da (mille) lire**
	da (meeleh) leereh
A single cone [*specify flavour, as above*]	**Un cono**
	oon cono
Two singles	**Due coni**
	dooeh conee
A double cone	**Un cono a due gusti**
	oon cono ah dooeh goostee
Two doubles	**Due coni a due gusti**
	dooeh conee ah dooeh goostee
A mixed cone	**Un cono misto**
	oon cono meesto
A tub	**Una coppa**
	oona cop-pa
A lollipop	**Un ghiacciolo**
	oon ghee-at-cholo
A packet of ...	**Un pacchetto di ...**
	oon pac-ket-to dee ...
100 grams of ...	**Cento grammi di ...**
	chento gram-mee dee ...
200 grams of ...	**Duecento grammi di ...**
	dooeh-chento gram-mee dee ...
chewing gum	cicles
	cheec-lez
chocolates	cioccolatini
	choc-colat-eenee
mints	caramelle alla menta
	caramel-leh al-la menta
sweets	caramelle
	caramel-leh
toffees	caramelle mu
	caramel-leh moo

[*For other essential expressions see 'Shop talk', p. 57.*]

In the supermarket

ESSENTIAL INFORMATION

- The place to ask for: [see p. 18]
  SUPERMERCATO   (supermarket)
  SUPERMERCATO-ALIMENTARI (food supermarket)
- Supermarket chains which can be found in most parts of Italy:
  COOP   STANDA
  PAM   UPIM
  GAROSCI
- Key instructions on signs in the shop:
  ENTRATA   (entrance)
  USCITA   (exit)
  VIETATO L'INGRESSO   (no entry)
  CASSA   (cash desk, check-out)
  OFFERTA SPECIALE   (special offer)
  CARRELLI   (trolleys)
- Opening times vary but are generally 9–12.30 and 3.30–7.30.
- For non-food items see 'Replacing equipment', p. 54.
- No need to say anything in a supermarket, but ask if you can't see what you want.

WHAT TO SAY

Excuse me, please	**Mi scusi, per favore**
	mee sco*o*zee pair fav-*oreh*
Where is ...	**Dov'è ...**
	dov-*eh* ...
the bread?	**il pane?**
	il p*a*n-eh
the butter?	**il burro?**
	il b*oo*rro
the cheese?	**il formaggio?**
	il form*a*d-jo
the chocolate?	**il cioccolato?**
	il choc-col*a*t-o
the coffee?	**il caffè?**
	il caf-feh
the cooking oil?	**l'olio per friggere?**
	l*o*l-yo pair fr*i*d-jereh

the fresh fish?	il pesce fresco
	il pesheh fresco
the fruit?	la frutta?
	la froot-ta
the jam?	la marmellata?
	la marmel-lat-ah
the meat?	la carne?
	la carneh
the milk?	il latte?
	il lat-teh
the mineral water?	l'acqua minerale?
	lacqua mineral-eh
the salt?	il sale?
	il sal-eh
the sugar?	lo zucchero?
	lo dzooc-kero
the tea?	il tè?
	il teh
the tinned fish?	il pesce in scatola?
	il pesheh in scat-ola
the tinned fruit?	la frutta sciroppata?
	la froot-ta sheerop-**pat-ah**
the vinegar?	l'aceto?
	lacheh-to
the wine?	il vino?
	il veeno
the yogurt?	lo yogurt?
	lo yogurt
the pasta?	la pasta?
	la pasta
the vegetable section?	il reparto verdura?
	il reparto vairdoo-**ra**
Where are ...	Dove sono ...
	dov-eh sonno ...
the biscuits?	i biscotti?
	ee beescot-tee
the crisps?	le patatine fritte?
	leh patateeneh freet-teh
the eggs?	le uova?
	leh wova
the frozen foods?	i surgelati?
	ee soor-jelat-ee

Where are . . .	Dove sono . . .
	dov-eh sonno . . .
the fruit juices?	i succhi di frutta?
	ee sooc-kee dee froot-ta
the seafoods?	i frutti di mare?
	ee froot-tee dee mar-eh
the soft drinks?	le analcoliche?
	leh an-alcol-eekeh
the sweets?	i dolci?
	ee dolchi
the tinned foods?	i cibi in scatola?
	ee cheebee in scat-ola

[For other essential expressions see 'Shop talk', p. 57.]

Picnic food

ESSENTIAL INFORMATION

- Key words to look for:
  SALUMERIA
  SALUMI   (delicatessen)
  GASTRONOMIA
- In these shops you can buy a wide variety of food such as ham, salami, cheese, olives, appetizers, sausages, and freshly made take-away dishes. Specialities differ from region to region.
- Weight guide:
  4–6 oz/150 g of prepared salad per two people, if eaten as a starter to substantial meal.
  3–4 oz/100 g of prepared salad per person, if to be eaten as the main part of a picnic-type meal.

WHAT TO SAY

One slice of . . .	Una fetta di . . .
	oona fet-ta dee . . .
Two slices of . . .	Due fette di . . .
	dooeh fet-teh dee . . .
roast beef	arrosto
	arrosto

roast pork	**arrosto di maiale**
	arrosto dee mah-yal-eh
tongue	**lingua**
	lín-gwa
veal with mayonnaise	**vitello tonnato**
	veetel-lo ton-nat-o
bacon	**pancetta**
	panchet-ta
salami (raw/cooked)	**salame (crudo/cotto)**
	salam-eh (croodo/cot-to)
ham (raw/cooked)	**prosciutto (crudo/cotto)**
	proshoot-to (croodo/cot-to)
meat loaf	**polpettone arrosto**
	polpet-toneh arrosto
100 grams of ...	**Cento grammi di ...**
	chento gram-mee dee ...
150 grams of ...	**Centocinquanta grammi di ...**
	chento-chin-quanta gram-mee dee ...
200 grams of ...	**Duecento grammi di ...**
	dooehchento gram-mee dee ...
300 grams of ...	**Trecento grammi di ...**
	treh-chento gram-mee dee ...
Russian salad	**insalata russa**
	insalat-ah roos-sa
seafood salad	**insalata di mare**
	insalat-ah dee mareh
tuna and olive salad	**insalata di tonno e olive**
	insalat-ah dee ton-no eh oleeveh
frankfurter salad	**insalata di würsteln**
	insalat-ah dee woorsteln
prawn salad	**insalata di gamberetti**
	insalat-ah dee gambairet-tee
rice salad	**insalata di riso**
	insalat-ah dee reezo

You might also like to try some of these:

olive verdi	green olives
oleeveh vairdee	
olive nere	black olives
oleeveh naireh	

olive nere al forno oleeveh *nai*reh al *forno*	baked black olives
olive verdi ripiene oleeveh *vai*rdee rip-yen-eh	stuffed green olives
funghetti sott'olio foong*het*-tee sot-*tol*-yo	mushrooms preserved in oil
peperoni sott'olio peper*onee* sot-*tol*-yo	peppers preserved in oil
peperoni arrosto peper*onee* arr*osto*	roasted peppers
peperoni ripieni peper*onee* rip-yen-ee	stuffed peppers
pomodori ripieni pomod*oree* rip-yen-ee	stuffed tomatoes
cipolle ripiene chip*ol*-leh rip-yen-eh	stuffed onions
melanzane in parmigiana melandz*an*-eh in parmij*an*-ah	aubergines cooked in tomato sauce and parmesan cheese
zucchini in carpione zooc-*kee*nee in carp-yoneh	courgettes cooked in oil and vinegar, sage and garlic
zucchini ripieni zuc-*kee*nee rip-yen-ee	stuffed courgettes
patatine fritte patat*een*eh freet-teh	crisps, freshly made daily
lasagne al forno laz*an*-yeh al *forno*	wide, flat noodles baked in a sauce of meat and bechamel
gnocchi alla romana n-*yoc*-kee al-la rom*an*-ah	small, flat semolina 'dumplings' with butter and parmesan cheese
cannelloni ripieni can-nel-*lonee* rip-yen-ee	large tubular pasta stuffed with meat, or spinach and cheese
gnocchi alla fontina n-*yoc*-kee al-la font*eena*	potato 'dumplings' with melted fontina cheese
torta di verdura *torta* dee vaird*oo*-ra	vegetable pie
torta pasqualina *torta* pasqwal*eena*	spinach, eggs and herbs in a puff pastry pie
parmigiano parmij*an*-o	parmesan, a hard, strong cheese used in cooking, usually grated
robiola rob-*yola*	a mild fresh white cheese made from ewe's milk
pecorino pecor*eeno*	a strong hard cheese, eaten fresh or grated when mature

ricotta ricot-ta	a soft white, very bland curd cheese made from ewe's milk
fontina font*eena*	a rich Alpine cheese usually melted in cooking
provolone provolo*neh*	a hard yellow cow's milk cheese displayed hanging up
gorgonzola gorgon-tz*ola*	a blue-veined cheese with a rich soft texture
mozzarella mot-tzar-*el*-la	a white flavourless curd cheese, should be eaten very fresh

[*For other essential expressions see 'Shop talk', p. 57*]

Fruit and vegetables

ESSENTIAL INFORMATION

- Key words to look for:
FRUTTA	(fruit)
VERDURA	(vegetables)
PRIMIZIE	(an indication of freshness)
ALIMENTARI	(grocer's and greengrocer's)
MERCATO	(market)
- If possible, buy fruit and vegetables in the market. where they are cheaper and fresher than in the shops. Open-air markets are held once or twice a week in most areas (or daily in large towns), usually in the mornings.
- It is customary for you to choose your own fruit and vegetables at the market (and in some shops) and for the stallholder to weigh them and price them. You must take your own shopping bag: paper and plastic bags are not normally provided.
- Weight guide: 1 kilo of potatoes is sufficient for six people for one meal.

WHAT TO SAY

½ kilo (1 lb) of ...	Mezzo chilo di ... med-dzo *keelo* dee ...
1 kilo of ...	Un chilo di ... oon *keelo* dee ...

2 kilos of ...	Due chili di ...
	dooeh keelee dee ...
apples	mele
	mel-eh
bananas	banane
	banan-eh
cherries	ciliegie
	chil-yeh-jeh
grapes (white/black)	uva (bianca/nera)
	oova (bee-anca/naira)
oranges	arance
	arancheh
pears	pere
	paireh
peaches	pesche
	peskeh
plums	prugne
	proon-yeh
strawberries	fragole
	fragoleh
A pineapple, please	Un ananas, per favore
	oon ananas pair fav-oreh
A grapefruit	Un pompelmo
	oon pompelmo
A melon	Un melone
	oon meloneh
A water melon	Un'anguria
	oon-angoo-ria
250 grams of ...	Duecentocinquanta grammi di ...
	dooeh-chento-chinquanta gram-mee dee ...
½ kilo of ...	Mezzo chilo di ...
	med-dzo keelo dee ...
1 kilo of ...	Un chilo di ...
	oon keelo dee ...
1½ kilos of ...	Un chilo e mezzo di ...
	oon keelo eh med-dzo dee ...
2 kilos of ...	Due chili di ...
	dooeh keelee dee ...
artichokes	carciofi
	carchof-ee

aubergines	melanzane
	melandzan-eh
carrots	carote
	carot-eh
courgettes	zucchini
	tzooc-keenee
green beans	fagiolini
	fad-joleenee
leeks	porri
	porree
mushrooms	funghi
	foonghee
onions	cipolle
	chipol-leh
peas	piselli
	peezel-lee
peppers (green/red)	peperoni (verdi/rossi)
	peperonee (vairdee/ros-see)
potatoes	patate
	patat-eh
spinach	spinaci
	speenachee
tomatoes	pomodori
	pomodoree
A bunch of ...	Un mazzetto di ...
	oon mat-tzet-to dee ...
parsley	prezzemolo
	pret-tzem-olo
radishes	rapanelli
	rapanel-lee
A head of garlic	Una testa d'aglio
	oona testa dal-yo
Some lettuce	Dell'insalata
	del-linsalat-ah
A cauliflower	Un cavolfiore
	oon cavol-feeoreh
A cabbage	Un cavolo
	oon cavolo
A stick of celery	Un sedano
	oon sedan-o
A cucumber	Un cetriolo
	oon chetree-olo

Like that, please **Come quello, per favore**
com-eh quel-lo pair fav-*oreh*

These are some fruit and vegetables which may not be familiar:

cachi	soft, sweet winter fruit, like a large
k*a*k-ee	tomato
nespole	medlars: small, slightly sour fruit,
n*e*spoleh	orange colour, juicy
cardi	cardoons: the top stalks of the
c*a*rdee	thistle artichoke
finocchi	fennels: crunchy vegetable with
feen*oc*-kee	aniseed flavour
radicchio rosso	small-leafed red salad with a slightly
rad*ee*c-kee r*o*s-so	bitter flavour

[*For other essential expressions see 'Shop talk', p. 57.*]

Meat

ESSENTIAL INFORMATION

- Key words to look for:
  MACELLAIO (butcher)
  MACELLERIA (butcher's)
- Butchers, especially in small towns and villages, often use a white sheet hung outside the shop as a sign.
- Weight guide: 4–6 oz/125–200 g of meat per person for one meal.
- The diagrams opposite are to help you make sense of labels on counters and supermarket displays, and decide which cut or joint to have. Translations do not help, and you don't need to say the Italian word involved.
- Mutton and lamb are only sold and eaten during the Easter period.

Beef Manzo

1 Stinco
2 Muscolo
3 Girello
4 Coscia, noce, rosa
5 Lombo, filetto
6 Costata
7 Guancia, testa
8 Collo
9 Polpa di spalla
10 Costato
11 Punta di petto
12 Pancia

Veal Vitello

1 Ossobuco
2 Cosciotto, magatello, noce
3 Codino
4 Lombata, nodini, costolette, scamone
5 Filetto
6 Copertina di spalla
7 Spalla, capello del prete, fusello
8 Testina
9 Collo
10 Fiocco di petto
11 Punta di petto
12 Pancetta

Pork Maiale

1 Testina
2 Coste, lombata, lonza, filetto
3 Spalla, prosciutto di spalla
4 Coscio, prosciutto di mezzo
5 Petto, pancetta
6 Cosciotto
7 Coscia, zampone
8 Piedino

Lamb, kid Agnello, Capretto

1 Testina, collo
2 Sella, costolette
3 Cosciotto
4 Spalla
5 Petto

WHAT TO SAY

For a joint, choose the type of meat and then say how many people
it is for:

Some beef, please	**Del manzo, per favore**
	del man-zo pair fav-oreh
Some lamb	**Dell'agnello**
	del-lan-yel-lo
Some pork	**Del maiale**
	del mah-yal-eh
Some veal	**Del vitello**
	del veetel-lo
A joint ...	**Un arrosto ...**
	oon arrosto ...
for two people	**per due persone**
	pair dooeh pairsoneh
for four people	**per quattro persone**
	pair quat-tro pairsoneh
for six people	**per sei persone**
	pair say pairsoneh

For steak, liver or heart, use the same idea:

Some steak, please	**Della bistecca, per favore**
	del-la beestec-ca pair fav-oreh
Some liver	**Del fegato**
	del feh-gat-o
Some kidneys	**Dei rognoni**
	day ron-yonee
Some heart	**Del cuore**
	del cworeh
Some sausages	**Delle salsicce**
	del-leh salseet-cheh
Some mince	**Della carne tritata**
	del-la carneh treetat-ah
for three people	**per tre persone**
	pair treh pairsoneh
for five people	**per cinque persone**
	pair chinqueh pairsoneh

For chops do it this way:

Two veal escalopes	**Due fettine di vitello**
	dooeh fet-*tee*neh dee veetel-lo
Three pork chops	**Tre braciole di maiale**
	treh brach*oleh* dee mayal-eh
Four lamb chops	**Quattro costolette d'agnello**
	quat-tro costolet-teh dan-yel-lo
Five beef chops	**Cinque fettine di manzo**
	*chin*queh fet-*tee*neh dee mandzo

You may also want:

A chicken	**Un pollo**
	oon pol-lo
A rabbit	**Un coniglio**
	oon coneel-yo
A tongue	**Una lingua**
	oona leengwa

Other essential expressions [*see also p. 57*]:

Please can you . . .	**Per favore potrebbe . . .**
	pair fav-*oreh* potreb-beh . . .
clean it?	**pulirlo?**
	pooleerlo
mince it?	**tritarlo?**
	treetarlo
dice it?	**tagliarlo a pezzetti?**
	tal-yarlo ah pet-tzet-tee
trim the fat?	**togliere il grasso?**
	tol-yereh il gras-so

Fish

ESSENTIAL INFORMATION

- The places to ask for are:
  PESCHERIA   (fish shop)
  MERCATO DEL PESCE   (fish market)
- Another key word to look for is FRUTTI DI MARE (shellfish).
- Large supermarkets usually have a fresh fish stall.
- Weight guide: 8 oz/250 g minimum per person for one meal of
  fish bought on the bone, i.e.
  ½ kilo/500 grams   for 2 people
  1 kilo   for 4 people
  1½ kilos   for 6 people

WHAT TO SAY

Purchase large fish and small shellfish by the weight:

½ kilo of . . .	Mezzo chilo di . . .
	med-dzo keelo dee . . .
1 kilo of . . .	Un chilo di . . .
	oon keelo dee . . .
1½ kilos of . . .	Un chilo e mezzo di . . .
	oon keelo eh med-dzo dee . . .
anchovies	acciughe
	at-choogeh
cod	merluzzo
	merloot-tzo
eel	anguilla
	angweel-la
mussels (*two names*)	muscoli/cozze
	moos-colee/cot-tzeh
octopus	polipo
	poleepo
oysters	ostriche
	ostreekeh
prawns	gamberi
	gamberee
red mullet	triglie
	treel-yeh

sardines	**sardine**
	sardeeneh
scampi	**scampi**
	scampee
shrimps	**gamberetti**
	gamberet-tee
small squid	**calamaretti**
	calamaret-tee
squid	**calamari**
	calama-ree

Some large fish can be purchased by the slice:

One slice of ...	**Una fetta di ...**
	oona fet-ta dee ...
Two slices of ...	**Due fette di ...**
	dooeh fet-teh dee ...
Six slices of ...	**Sei fette di ...**
	say fet-teh dee ...
dogfish	**palombo**
	palombo
cod	**merluzzo**
	merloot-tzo
swordfish	**pescespada**
	pesheh-spad-ah
fresh tuna	**tonno fresco**
	ton-no fresco

For some shellfish and 'frying pan' fish, specify the number you want:

A crab, please	**Un granchio, per favore**
	oon grankeeo pair fav-oreh
A lobster	**Un'aragosta**
	oonaragosta
A red mullet	**Una triglia**
	oona treel-ya
A cod	**Un merluzzo**
	oon merloot-tzo
A trout	**Una trota**
	oona trot-a
A sole	**Una sogliola**
	oona sol-yola

A dory [*expensive*]	**Un'orata** oonorat-ah
A bass [*expensive*]	**Un branzino** oon brandzeeno
A mullet	**Un cefalo** oon chefalo

Other essential expressions [*see also p. 57*]:

Please can you ...	**Per favore potrebbe ...** pair fav-oreh potreb-beh ...
take the heads off?	**tagliare le teste?** tal-yar-eh leh testeh
clean them?	**pulirli?** pooleerlee
fillet them?	**tagliarli in filetti?** tal-yarlee in filet-tee

Eating and drinking out

Ordering a drink

ESSENTIAL INFORMATION

● The places to ask for [see p. 18]:
  BAR
  BAR-PASTICCERIA   (drinks and cakes)
  CAFFÈ
  BIRRERIA   (beer and snacks)
● By law, the price list of drinks (LISTINO PREZZI) must be displayed somewhere in the bar.
● There is waiter service in some cafés, but you can drink at the bar or counter if you wish (cheaper). In this case you should first pay at the cash desk (CASSA) and then take the receipt (scontrino) to the bar and give your order.
● Service is normally included in the bill (servizio compreso) but if not should be 10% to 15%.
● Bars and cafés serve both non-alcoholic and alcoholic drinks. There are no licensing hours, and children are allowed in.
● Italians drink a range of aperitifs (aperitivi) and digestives (digestivi). Their names vary from region to region. Most of the aperitifs are types of vermouth – red or white, sweet or dry – made by different firms such as Campari, Punt e Mes and Martini. The digestives can be made from almonds, fruit, or herbs and are often thick and syrupy.

WHAT TO SAY

I'll have . . . please	Prendo, per favore . . .
	prendo pair fav-*oreh* . . .
a black coffee (small and strong)	un caffè
	oon caf-*feh*
a black coffee (less strong)	un caffè lungo
	oon caf-*feh* loong-go
a coffee with a dash of cream	un caffè macchiato
	oon caf-*feh* mac-kee-*at*-o
a milky coffee (breakfast)	un caffelatte
	oon caf-eh-*lat*-teh

I'll have . . . please	**Prendo, per favore . . .** prendo pair fav-*oreh* . . .
a frothy white coffee	**un capuccino** oon capooch*eeno*
a tea	**un tè** oon teh
with milk	**al latte** al *lat*-teh
with lemon	**al limone** al leem*oneh*
a glass of milk	**un bicchiere di latte** oon beec-kee-*air*eh dee l*at*-teh
a hot chocolate	**una cioccolata calda** oona choc-col*at*-ah c*alda*
a mineral water	**una minerale** oona mineral-eh
an iced coffee	**una granita di caffè** oona gran*eeta* dee c*af-feh*
a lemonade	**una limonata** oona leemon*at*-a
a fresh lemon juice	**una spremuta di limone** oona sprem*oota* dee leem*oneh*
a Coca Cola	**una Coca Cola** oona coca cola
an orangeade	**un'aranciata** oonaranch*at*-a
a fresh orange juice	**una spremuta d'arancia** oona sprem*oota* dar*ancha*
a fresh grapefruit juice	**una spremuta di pompelmo** oona sprem*oota* dee pomp*elmo*
a pineapple juice	**un succo di frutta all'ananas** oon s*ooc*-co dee fr*oot*-ta al-l*ananas*
a peach juice	**un succo di frutta alla pesca** oon s*ooc*-co dee fr*oot*-ta al-la p*esca*
a lager	**una birra** oona b*eerra*
a dark beer	**una birra scura** oona b*eerra* sc*oo*-ra
A glass of . . .	**Un bicchiere di . . .** oon beec-kee-*air*eh dee . . .
Two glasses of . . .	**Due bicchieri di . . .** d*ooeh* beec-kee-*air*ee dee . . .

red wine	vino rosso
	v*ee*no ros-so
white wine	vino bianco
	v*ee*no bee-*a*nco
rosé wine	rosé
	roz*e*h
dry	secco
	s*e*c-co
sweet	dolce
	d*o*lcheh
A bottle of ...	Una bottiglia di ...
	oona bot-t*ee*l-ya dee ...
sparkling wine	spumante
	spoom*a*nteh
champagne	champagne
	shamp*a*n-yeh
A whisky	Un whisky
	oon w*i*sky
with ice	con ghiaccio
	con ghee-*a*t-cho
with water	con acqua
	con *a*cqua
with soda	con seltz
	con s*e*ltz
A gin	Un gin
	oon jeen
and tonic	con tonico
	con t*o*n-eeco
with lemon	con limone
	con leem*o*neh
A brandy	Un cognac
	oon c*o*n-yac

Other essential expressions:

Miss! [*this does not sound abrupt in Italian*]	Signorina!
	seen-yor*ee*na
Waiter!	Cameriere!
	cameree-*ai*reh
The bill, please!	Il conto per favore!
	il conto pair fav-*o*reh
How much does that come to?	Quanto fa?
	qu*a*nto f*a*

Is service included?   **Il servizio è compreso?**
                        il sairv*i*tzio eh compra*i*zo

Where is the toilet, please?   **Dov'è il bagno per favore?**
                        dov-*eh* il ba*n*-yo pair fav-*o*reh

Ordering a snack

ESSENTIAL INFORMATION

● Look for a café or bar with these signs:

  PANINI
  TRAMEZZINI   ⎤   (sandwiches)
  TOASTS   ⎦

  TAVOLA CALDA ⎤
  PIZZE   ⎟
  PIZZERIA   ⎟   (hot snacks)
  BIRRERIA   ⎦

● In some regions mobile vans sell hot snacks.
● In bars, if you want to eat your snack at the counter you need to pay first at the cash desk and then hand the receipt to the waiter behind the bar.
● For cakes, see p. 62.
  For ice-cream, see p. 64.
  For picnic-type snacks, see p. 68.
  For ordering a drink, see p. 81.
● Small sandwiches called **tramezzini** are popular snacks and are made with a variety of fillings. It is best to point to the ones you fancy.
● If olives, anchovies, crisps and nuts are available in bars, their price will normally be included with the drinks.

WHAT TO SAY

I'll have ... please   **Prendo, per favore ...**
                        pr*e*ndo pair fav-*o*reh ...

  a cheese roll   **un panino al formaggio**
                        oon pan*ee*no al form*a*d-jo

  a ham roll   **un panino al prosciutto**
                        oon pan*ee*no al prosh*oo*t-to

I'll have . . . please	Prendo, per favore . . .
	prendo pair fav-*oreh* . . .
a salami roll	un panino al salame
	oon pan*ee*no al sal*am*-eh
a sandwich (like that)	un tramezzino (così)
	oon tramed-dz*ee*no (coz*ee*)
a pizza	una pizza
	oona p*ee*t-tza

These are some other snacks you may like to try:

una pizzetta al pomodoro	small tomato pizza, usually eaten
oona pit-*tzet*-ta al pomodoro	cold
una focaccia	a savoury bread, similar to pizza but
oona foc*at*-cha	without tomato spread
una focaccina al prosciutto	a ham sandwich made with **focaccia**
oona focat-ch*ee*na al	bread
prosh*oot*-to	
un toast (al prosciutto e	a toasted sandwich, normally made
formaggio)	with ham and cheese
oon tost (al prosh*oot*-to eh	
form*ad*-djo)	

[*For other essential expressions see 'Ordering a drink', p. 83.*]

In a restaurant

ESSENTIAL INFORMATION

- The place to ask for: **un ristorante** [*see p. 18*]
- You can eat at all these places:

  RISTORANTE
  TRATTORIA (cheaper)
  ALBERGO (hotel – often a fixed menu)
  PENSIONE (mainly residents – fixed menu)
  ROSTICCERIA
  PIZZERIA
  BIRRERIA (hot snacks)
  TAVOLA CALDA

- Menus are always displayed outside the larger restaurants and that is the *only* way to judge if a place is right for your needs.
- Some smaller restaurants do not have a written menu and you must ask the waiter what is available.
- Self-service restaurants are rare.
- Service (of 10% to 15%) is always included on the bill, but an extra tip is usually welcome.
- Restaurants are now obliged, by law, to give receipts, and you should insist on this.
- In the south of Italy the lunch break is longer than in the north, and dinner is eaten later in the evening.

WHAT TO SAY

May I book a table?	**Potrei prenotare un tavolo?**
	potr*ay* prenotar-eh oon *tavolo*
I've booked a table	**Ho prenotato un tavolo**
	o prenot*at*-o oon *tavolo*
A table ...	**Un tavolo ...**
	oon *tavolo* ...
for one	**per una persona**
	pair *oona* pairs*ona*
for three	**per tre persone**
	pair tr*eh* pairs*oneh*
The à la carte menu, please	**Il menú alla carta, per favore**
	il men*oo* al-la c*a*rta pair fav-*oreh*

The fixed price menu	Il menú a prezzo fisso
	il men*oo* ah pret-tzo fís-so
The (8,000) lira menu	Il menú da (ottomila) lire
	il men*oo* da (*ot*-tomeela) leereh
The tourist menu	Il menú turistico
	il men*oo* toor*í*stico
Today's special menu	I piatti del giorno
	ee pee-*at*-tee del jorno
What's this, please? [*point to menu*]	Che cos'è questo, per favore?
	keh coz-*eh* questo pair fav-*oreh*
A carafe of wine, please	Una caraffa di vino, per favore
	oona car*af*-fa dee veeno pair fav-*oreh*
A quarter (25 cc)	Un quarto
	oon qu*aar*to
A half (50 cc)	Un mezzo litro
	oon med-dzo leetro
A glass	Un bicchiere
	oon beec-kee-*ai*reh
A bottle	Una bottiglia
	oona bot-teel-ya
A half-bottle	Una mezza bottiglia
	oona med-dza bot-teel-ya
A litre	Un litro
	oon leetro
Red/white/rosé/house wine	Vino rosso/bianco/rosé/della casa
	veeno ros-so/bee-*anco*/roz*eh*/del-la c*aza*
Some more bread, please	Ancora del pane, per favore
	ancora del p*an*-eh pair fav-*oreh*
Some more wine	Ancora del vino
	ancora del veeno
Some oil	Dell'olio
	del-l*ol*-yo
Some vinegar	Dell'aceto
	del-lach*eto*
Some salt	Del sale
	del s*al*-eh
Some pepper	Del pepe
	del peh-peh
Some water	Dell'acqua
	del-l*acqua*

How much does that come to?	Quanto fa?
	quanto fa
Is service included?	Il servizio è compreso?
	il sairvitzio eh compraiz-o
Where is the toilet, please?	Dov'è il bagno, per favore?
	dov-eh il ban-yo pair fav-oreh
Miss! [this does not sound abrupt in Italian]	Signorina!
	seen-yoreena
Waiter!	Cameriere!
	cameree-aireh
The bill, please	Il conto, per favore
	il conto pair fav-oreh
May I have a receipt?	Potrei avere una ricevuta?
	potray avaireh oona reechevoota

Key words for courses, as seen on some menus

[Only ask this question if you want the waiter to remind you of the choice.]

What have you got in the way of . . .	Che cosa avete come . . .
	keh coza avet-eh com-eh . . .
STARTERS?	ANTIPASTI?
	antipastee
SOUP?	MINESTRE?
	minestreh
EGG DISHES?	UOVA?
	wova
FISH?	PESCE?
	pesheh
MEAT?	CARNE?
	carneh
GAME?	SELVAGGINA?
	selvad-jeena
FOWL?	POLLAME?
	pol-lam-eh
VEGETABLES?	CONTORNO?
	contorno
CHEESE?	FORMAGGI?
	formad-jee
FRUIT?	FRUTTA?
	froot-ta
ICE-CREAM?	GELATI?
	jelat-ee

DESSERT?   DOLCI?
                            dolchee

[*'Pasta', spaghetti, etc., are part of the MINESTRE course, see p. 93.*]

UNDERSTANDING THE MENU

● You will find the names of the principal ingredients of most dishes
  on these pages:

  Starters p. 68   Fruit p. 72
  Meat p. 74   Cheese p. 70
  Fish p. 78   Ice-cream p. 64
  Vegetables p. 73   Dessert p. 62

  Used together with the following lists of cooking and menu terms,
  they should help you to decode the menu.

● *Remember*, dishes vary considerably from region to region in
  Italy: a dish with the same name, e.g. gnocchi alla Romana (pasta
  'dumplings' Roman style), might be cooked in a different way in
  Rome from Milan – or even from one restaurant to another in the
  same city. Also, the same dish might appear on menus all over
  Italy with a different name in each region! If in doubt, always ask
  the waiter.

● These cooking and menu terms are for understanding only – not
  for speaking.

Cooking and menu terms

affumicato	smoked
all'aglio e olio	with oil and garlic
agrodolce	sweet-sour
arrosto	roast
al basilico	with basil
ben cotto	well cooked
con besciamella	with bechamel sauce
in bianco	boiled, with no sauce
bollito	boiled/stewed
alla bolognese	Bolognese style
brasato	cooked in wine
al burro	cooked in butter
alla cacciatora	cooked in tomato sauce
al cartoccio	baked wrapped in foil
alla casalinga	homely style
al civet	marinated and cooked in wine

cotto	cooked (as opposed to raw)
crudo	raw
al dente	not overcooked, firm texture
dorato	slightly fried (golden)
alle erbe	with herbs
da farsi	to be prepared
ai ferri	grilled without oil
alla fiorentina	Florentine style
alla fonduta	with fondue
al forno	baked
fritto	fried
in gelatina	in savoury jelly
grattuggiato	grated; baked in cheese sauce
alla griglia	grilled on the fire
imbottiti	stuffed
lesso	boiled
in maionese	in/with mayonnaise
alle mandorle	with almonds
alla marinara	with seafood
al marsala	with Marsala wine
alla milanese	fried in egg and breadcrumbs
alla napoletana	Neopolitan style
all'origano	with oregano (herb)
in padella	cooked and served in a frying pan
al pangrattato	with breadcrumbs
alla panna	cooked in cream
al parmigiano	with parmesan cheese
al pecorino	with pecorino cheese
al pesto	with basil and garlic sauce
alla pizzaiola	with tomato sauce and cheese
al prezzemolo	with parsley
ragù	rich tomato and meat sauce for pasta
alla ricotta	with ricotta cheese
ripieno	stuffed
alla romana	Roman style
al rosmarino	with rosemary
salsa	sauce
salsa verde	parsley and garlic sauce
in salmì	cooked in oil, vinegar and herbs
al sangue	rare (steak, etc.)
alla siciliana	Sicilian style

spiedini	skewers
allo spiedo	on the spit
stufato	stew
al sugo	cooked in sauce
trifolato	cooked with tomato and parsley
in umido	steamed; stewed
alla veneziana	Venetian style
alle vongole	with clam (shellfish) sauce
allo zabaglione	with eggs, sugar and Marsala wine
zuppa	soup

Further words to help you to understand the menu:

abbacchio	young, spring lamb
amaretti	macaroons
anguilla	eel
animelle	sweetbreads
anitra	duck
baccalà	dried cod
bagna cauda	raw vegetables dipped in sauce of hot oil, garlic, anchovies and cream
bistecca alla fiorentina	T-bone steak
braciole	chops
brodo	broth
budino	like crème caramel; pudding
cacciagione	game
capperi	capers
capretto	kid
capriolo	deer
cassata	ice-cream cake with dried fruit
cervella	brains
cinghiale	boar
coppa	very lean bacon; cup (of ice-cream)
costate	large chops
costolette	small chops
cotechino	large pork sausage
crema	custard cream; cream soup
crostata	fruit or jam tart
crostini	small pieces of fried bread
fagiano	pheasant
fagioli	fresh or dried beans

fave	broad or butter beans
fegatini	chicken livers
fettine	small tender steaks
filetti	fillets
fragole di bosco	wild strawberries
frittata	omelette
frittelle	fritters
fritto misto	mixed fried meats
fritto di pesce	mixed fried fish
frutti di mare	shellfish
gelati	ice-cream
granita	water ice
grissini	crispy bread sticks
involtini	slices of meat, stuffed and rolled
lepre	hare
limone	lemon
lombata	sirloin
macedonia	fruit salad
mandorle	almonds
minestrone	vegetable soup
mortadella	large mild salami
ossibuchi	dish of shin of veal
pancetta	bacon
panna	cream
pasta asciutta	general name of cooked pasta
pasta frolla	rich shortcrust pastry
pasta sfogliata	puff pastry
peperonata	stew of green and red peppers
peperoncini	chili peppers
pernice	partridge
petti di pollo/tacchino	chicken/turkey breasts
piccata	small veal slices
pignoli	pine nuts
pinzimonio	raw vegetables to dip in oil
polpette	meatballs
prosciutto di Parma	raw ham from Parma
quaglia	quail
riso	rice
risotto	rice cooked in sauce
rolata	meat loaf stuffed with herbs
salame all'aglio	garlic sausage
salsiccia	sausage

saltimbocca alla romana	fried veal with ham and rosemary
scaloppine	small veal slices
semifreddo	ice-cream with biscuits
seppie	cuttle-fish
spezzatino	stew
stracciatella	hot broth with beaten egg
stracotto	beef stew with vegetables
tacchino	turkey
tartuffi	truffles
torta	cake
trippa	tripe
uccelli	small birds (e.g. thrushes)
uova	eggs
vongole	clams, cockles
zampone	pig's trotter stuffed with chopped, seasoned meat
zuppa inglese	chocolate trifle
zuppa pavese	broth, lightly boiled egg and cheese

Types of pasta

agnolini/agnolotti	like ravioli
cannelloni	large tubular pasta, often stuffed
cappelletti	stuffed pasta rings
conchiglie	shell-shaped pasta
ditali	short tubular pasta
farfalle	butterfly-shaped pasta
fettuccine	narrow ribbons of pasta
gnocchi	small potato or semolina 'dumplings'
lasagne	wide flat pasta
maccheroni	large spaghetti with hole in middle
pasta asciutta	general term for cooked pasta
pasta in brodo	small shapes of pasta in broth
pizza	flat 'bread' spread with tomato
polenta	porridge of maize flour
ravioli	stuffed square-shaped pasta
rigatoni	large-grooved tubular pasta
spaghetti	long, thin, round pasta
tagliatelle	narrow ribbon pasta
tortellini	stuffed pasta rings
vermicelli	very thin spaghetti, 'little worms'
ziti	tubular-shaped pasta

Health

ESSENTIAL INFORMATION

- For details of reciprocal health agreements between your country and the country you are visiting, visit your local Department of Health office at least one month before leaving, or ask your travel agent.
- In addition, it is preferable to purchase a medical insurance policy through the travel agent, a broker or a motoring organization.
- The Italian state medical insurance is called INAM.
- Take your own 'first line' first aid kit with you.
- For minor disorders and treatment at a drug store, see p. 41.
- For asking the way to a doctor, dentist, drug store or Health and Social Security Office (for reimbursement) see pg. 20.
- Once in Italy decide a definite plan of action in case of serious illness: communicate your problem to a near neighbour, the receptionist or someone you see regularly. You are then dependent on that person helping you obtain treatment.
- To find a doctor in an emergency, look for:
  medici (in the Yellow Pages of the telephone directory)
  AMBULATORIO   (surgery)
  PRONTO SOCCORSO   (casualty department, first aid)
  H
  OSPEDALE]   (hospital)
- Dial 113 for an emergengy ambulance service.

What's the matter?

I have a pain in my ...	Mi fa male ... mee fa mal-eh ...
ankle	la caviglia la caveel-ya
arm	il braccio il brat-cho
back	la schiena la skee-ehna
bladder	la vescica la vesheeca
bowels	l'intestino lintesteeno

breast	**il seno**
	il sen-o
chest	**il torace**
	il toracheh
ear	**l'orecchio**
	lorec-keeo
eye	**l'occhio**
	loc-yo
foot	**il piede**
	il pee-ehdeh
head	**la testa**
	la testa
heel	**il calcagno**
	il calcan-yo
jaw	**la mandibola**
	la mandeebola
kidney	**il rene**
	il reh-neh
leg	**la gamba**
	la gamba
lung	**il polmone**
	il polmoneh
neck	**il collo**
	il col-lo
penis	**il pene**
	il peh-neh
shoulder	**la spalla**
	la spal-la
stomach (abdomen)	**lo stomaco (addome)**
	lo stom-aco (ad-domeh)
testicle	**il testicolo**
	il testeecolo
throat	**la gola**
	la gola
vagina	**la vagina**
	la vajeena
wrist	**il polso**
	il polso
I have a pain here [*point*]	**Ho un dolore qui**
	o oon doloreh quee
I have toothache	**Ho male a un dente**
	o mal-eh ah oon denteh

I have broken ...
Ho rotto ...
o *rot*-to ...

　my dentures
　la dentiera
　la dentee-*ai*ra

　my glasses
　gli occhiali
　l-*yee* oc-kee-*al*-ee

I have lost ...
Ho perso ...
o *pair*so ...

　my contact lenses
　le lenti a contatto
　leh *len*tee ah con*tat*-to

　a filling
　un'otturazione
　oonot-too-ratzi*o*neh

My child is ill
Mio/a figlio/a è
　　ammalato/a*
mee-o/ah f*ee*l-yo/ah eh
　　am-mal*at*-o/ah

He/She has a pain in
　his/her ...
　ankle [see list above]
Ha un dolore ...
ah oon dol*o*reh ...
alla caviglia
al-la cav*ee*l-ya

How bad is it?

I'm ill
Sto male
sto m*a*l-eh

It's urgent
È urgente
eh oorj*en*teh

It's serious
È grave
eh gr*a*v-eh

It's not serious
Non è grave
non eh gr*a*v-eh

It hurts
Fa male
fa m*a*l-eh

It hurts a lot
Fa molto male
fa m*o*lto m*a*l-eh

It doesn't hurt much
Non fa troppo male
non fa tr*o*p-po m*a*l-eh

The pain occurs ...
Il dolore si ripete ...
il dol*o*reh see rip*et*-eh ...

　every quarter of an hour
　ogni quarto d'ora
　*o*n-yee qw*aa*rto d*o*ra

*For boys use 'o', for girls use 'a'.

every half-hour	ogni mezz'ora
	on-yee med-dz*ora*
every hour	ogni ora
	on-yee *ora*
every day	ogni giorno
	on-yee jorno
most of the time	quasi sempre
	qu*a*-zee sempreh
I've had it for ...	L'ho da ...
	lo da ...
one hour/one day	un'ora/un giorno
	oon*ora*/oon jorno
two hours/two days	due ore/due giorni
	dooeh *oreh*/dooeh jornee
It's a ...	È ...
	eh ...
sharp pain	un dolore acuto
	oon doloreh ac*ooto*
dull ache	un dolore sordo
	oon doloreh sordo
nagging pain	un dolore continuo
	oon doloren cont*inoo-o*
I feel ...	Mi sento ...
	mee sento ...
weak	debole
	d*eh*-boleh
feverish	la febbre
	la f*eb*-breh
I feel ...	Ho ...
	o ...
dizzy	le vertigini
	leh vairt*ee*jeen*ee*
sick	la nausea
	la n*a*-oozeh-ah

Already under treatment for something else?

I take ... regularly [*show*]	Prendo regolarmente ...
	prendo regolarment*eh* ...
this medicine	questa medicina
	questa medich*eena*
these pills	queste pillole
	questeh p*eel*-loleh

I have ...   **Ho ...**
                                    o ...

  a heart condition   **mal di cuore**
                                    mal dee cworeh

  haemorrhoids   **le emorroidi**
                                    leh em-orroydee

  rheumatism   **i reumatismi**
                                    ee reh-oomatismee

I'm ...   **Sono ...**
                                    sonno ...

  diabetic   **diabetico/a***
                                    dee-abet-eeco/a

  asthmatic   **asmatico/a***
                                    azmat-eeco/a

  pregnant   **incinta**
                                    eencheenta

  allergic to (penicillin) **allergico/a* alla**
                                    (penicillina)
                                    al-lairjeeco/ah al-la
                                    (penicheel-leena)

Other essential expressions

Please can you help?   **Mi può aiutare per**
                                    favore?
                                    mee poo-o ayootar-eh pair
                                    fav-oreh

A doctor, please   **Un dottore, per favore**
                                    oon dot-toreh pair fav-oreh

A dentist   **Un dentista**
                                    oon denteesta

I don't speak Italian   **Non parlo italiano**
                                    non parlo italian-o

What time does ... arrive?   **A che ora arriva ... ?**
                                    ah keh ora arreeva ...

  the doctor   **il dottore**
                                    il dot-toreh

  the dentist   **il dentista**
                                    il denteesta

*Men use 'o' women use 'a'.

From the doctor: key sentences to understand:

Take this ...	**Prenda questo ...**
	prenda questo ...
every day/hour	**ogni giorno/ora**
	on-yee jorno/ora
twice/four times a day	**due/quattro volte al giorno**
	d*oo*eh/qu*a*t-tro volteh al jorno
Stay in bed	**Stia a letto**
	st*ee*-ah ah l*et*-to
Don't travel ...	**Non viaggi ...**
	non vee-*a*d-jee ...
for ... days/weeks	**per ... giorni/settimane**
	pair ... jornee/set-tim*a*n-*eh*
You must go to hospital	**Deve andare in ospedale**
	d*e*v-eh and*a*r-eh in osped-*a*l-*eh*

Problems: complaints, loss, theft

ESSENTIAL INFORMATION

- Problems with:
  camping facilities, see p. 35
  household appliances, see p. 54
  health, see p. 94
  the car, see p. 108
- If the worst comes to the worst, find the police station. To ask the way, see p. 18.
- Look for:
  CARABINIERI ⎤
  POLIZIA ⎦   (police)
  VIGILI URBANI   (traffic wardens)
  QUESTURA   (police station)
- If you lose your passport go to your nearest Consulate.
- In an emergency, dial 113 for fire and police.

COMPLAINTS

I bought this ...	**Ho comprato questo ...**
	o comprat-o questo ...
today	**oggi**
	od-jee
yesterday	**ieri**
	yeh-ree
on Monday [see p. 132]	**lunedí**
	loon-edee
It's no good	**Non va bene**
	non va ben-eh
Look	**Guardi**
	goo-ardee
Here [point]	**Qui**
	quee
Can you ...	**Potrebbe ...**
	potreb-be ...
change it?	**cambiarlo?**
	cambee-arlo
mend it?	**aggiustarlo?**
	ad-joostarlo
Here's the receipt	**Ecco la ricevuta**
	ec-co la reechevoota
Can I have a refund?	**Mi può rimborsare?**
	mee poo-o rimborsar-eh
Can I see the manager?	**Posso vedere il direttore?**
	pos-so ved-aireh il diret-toreh

LOSS
[See also 'Theft' below; the lists are interchangeable.]

I have lost ...	Ho perso ...
	o pairso ...
my bag	la borsa
	la borsa
my bracelet	**il braccialetto**
	il brat-chalet-to
my camera	**la macchina fotografica**
	la mac-keena fotograf-eeca
my car keys	**le chiavi della macchina**
	leh kee-ahv-ee del-la mac-keena

my car logbook	**il libretto della macchina**
	il libret-to del-la mac-keena
my driving licence	**la patente**
	la patenteh
my insurance certificate	**il certificato dell'assicurazione**
	il chairtee-ficat-o del-las-sicoo-ratzioneh
my jewellery	**i gioielli**
	ee joyel-lee
everything!	**tutto!**
	toot-to

THEFT
[*See also 'Loss' above; the lists are interchangeable.*]

Someone has stolen . . .	**Qualcuno mi ha rubato . . .**
	qualcoono mee ah roobat-o . . .
my car	**la macchina**
	la mac-keena
my car radio	**la radio della macchina**
	la rad-yo del-la mac-keena
my keys	**le chiavi**
	leh kee-ahv-ee
my money	**i soldi**
	ee soldee
my necklace	**la collana**
	la col-lan-ah
my passport	**il passaporto**
	il pas-saporto
my radio	**la radio**
	la rad-yo
my tickets	**i biglietti**
	ee beel-yet-tee
my travellers' cheques	**i travellers cheques**
	ee travellairs sheck
my wallet	**il portafoglio**
	il portafol-yo
my watch	**l'orologio**
	lorolodjo
my luggage	**i bagagli**
	ee bagal-yee

LIKELY REACTIONS: key words to understand

| Wait | **Aspetti**
aspet-tee |
| When? | **Quando?**
quando |
| Where? | **Dove?**
dov-eh |
| Name? | **Il suo nome?**
il soo-o nom-eh |
| Address? | **L'indirizzo?**
lindireet-tzo |
| I can't help you | **Non posso aiutarla**
non pos-so ayootarla |
| Nothing to do with me | **Non posso farci nulla**
non pos-so farchee nool-la |

The post office

ESSENTIAL INFORMATION

● To find a post office, see p. 18.
● Key words to look for:
  POSTA
  POSTE E TELEGRAFI (PT)
  POSTE-TELECOMUNICAZIONI (PTT)
● It is best to buy stamps at the smoke shop. Only go to the post office for more complicated transactions, like telegrams.
● See p. 47 for sign indicating smoke shop.
● Letter boxes are usually red.
● For poste restante you should show your passport at the counter marked **FERMO POSTA** in the main post office, and pay a small charge.

WHAT TO SAY

To England, please   **Per l'Inghilterra, per favore**
                       pair ling-eeltairra pair fav-oreh
[*Hand letters, cards or parcels over the counter.*]

To Australia	**Per l'Australia**
	pair la-oostral-ya
To the United States	**Per gli Stati Uniti**
	pair l-yee stat-ee ooneetee

[*For other countries see p. 136.*]

How much is ...	**Quanto costa spedire ...**
	quanto costa sped-eereh ...
this parcel (to Canada)?	**questo pacco (in Canada)?**
	questo pac-co (in canada)
a letter (to Australia)?	**una lettera (in Australia)?**
	oona let-tera (in ah-oostral-ya)
a post card (to England)?	**una cartolina (in Inghilterra)?**
	oona cartoleena (in ing-eeltairra)
Air mail	**Via aerea**
	vee-ah ah-aireh-ah
Surface mail	**Via normale**
	vee-ah normal-eh
One stamp, please	**Un francobollo, per favore**
	oon francobol-lo pair fav-oreh
Two stamps	**Due francobolli**
	dooeh francobol-lee
One (220) lira stamp	**Un francobollo da (duecento-venti) lire**
	oon francobol-lo da (dooeh-chento ventee) leereh
I'd like to send a telegram	**Vorrei spedire un telegramma**
	vorray sped-eereh oon telegram-ma

Telephoning

ESSENTIAL INFORMATION

- Unless you read and speak Italian well, it's best not to make telephone calls by yourself. Go to the main post office and write the town and number you want on a piece of paper. Add **con preavviso** if you want a person-to-person call, or **spese a carico del ricevente** if you want to reverse the charges.
- Telephone boxes are grey or yellow. You will find public telephones in most bars; look for this sign.

- To ask the way to a public telephone, see p. 21
- To use a public telephone, you have to buy a special coin called a **GETTONE** (sold in bars, smoke shops, post offices and some newsstands).
  For local calls **(CHIAMATE URBANE)**, you must insert the **gettone** and wait for the dial tone, before dialing.
  For longer distance calls **(CHIAMATE INTERURBANE)** at least **six gettoni** should be inserted before dialing.
- To call the UK using STD **(TELESELEZIONE)** dial the code 0044 then the number (less any initial O).
- For the USA you call the international operator **(ITALCABLE)**, dial 170.

WHAT TO SAY

Where can I make a telephone call?	Dove posso fare una telefonata?
	dov-eh pos-so far-eh oona telefonat-ah
Local/abroad	Locale/all'estero
	local-eh/al-lestero
I'd like this number ...	Vorrei questo numero ...
[show number]	vorray questo noomero ...
in England	in Inghilterra
	in ing-eeltairra
in Canada	in Canada
	in canada
in the USA	negli Stati Uniti
	nel-yee stat-ee ooneetee
[For other countries see p. 136.]	
Can you dial it for me, please?	Può farmi il numero, per favore?
	poo-o farmee il noomero pair fav-oreh
How much is it?	Quanto Le devo?
	quanto leh dev-o
Hello!	Pronto!
	pronto
May I speak to ... ?	Posso parlare con ... ?
	pos-so parlar-eh con
Extension ...	Interno ...
	intairno ...
I'm sorry, I don't speak Italian	Mi dispiace, non parlo italiano
	mee dispi-ah-cheh non parlo italian-o
Do you speak English?	Parla inglese?
	parla inglaizeh
Thank you, I'll phone back	Grazie, ritelefonerò
	gratzee-eh reetelefonero
Good-bye	A rivederci
	ah reevedairchee

LIKELY REACTIONS

That's (1,500) lira	**Fa (millecinquecento) lire** fa (meel-leh chinqueh-chento) leereh
Cabin number (3) [*For numbers see p. 128.*]	**Cabina numero (tre)** cabeena noomero (treh)
Don't hang up	**Attenda** at-tenda
I'm trying to connect you	**Cerco di collegarla** chairco dee col-legarla
You're through	**Parli pure** parlee poor-eh
There's a delay	**C'è un ritardo** cheh oon reetardo
I'll try again	**Proverò ancora** provero ancora

Changing checks and money

ESSENTIAL INFORMATION

- Finding your way to a bank or exchange bureau, see p. 19.
- Look for these words on buildings:
  - **BANCA**
  - **BANCO**
  - **INSTITUTO BANCARIO** ⎫ (bank)
  - **CASSA DI RISPARMIO** ⎭
  - **CAMBIO VALUTE** (change bureau)
- To cash your normal checks, exactly as at home use your credit card where you see the Eurocheque sign. Write in English.
- Have your passport handy.

WHAT TO SAY

I'd like to cash ...	**Vorrei incassare ...**
	vorr*ay* incas-s*ar*-eh ...
this travellers' cheque	**questo travellers cheque**
	questo travellairs sh*eck*
these travellers' cheques	**questi travellers cheques**
	quest*ee* travellairs sh*eck*
this cheque	**questo assegno**
	questo as-sen-yo
I'd like to change this into Italian lira	**Vorrei cambiare questi soldi** **in lire italiane**
	vorr*ay* cambi-*ar*-eh questee sold*ee* in l*ee*reh italian-eh
Here's ...	**Ecco ...**
	ec-co ...
my banker's card	**la mia carta assegni**
	la m*ee*-ah carta as-sen-y*ee*
my passport	**il mio passaporto**
	il m*ee*-o pas-saporto

For excursions into neighbouring countries:

I'd like to change this ... [*show bank notes*]	**Vorrei cambiare questi soldi ...**
	vorr*ay* cambi-*ar*-eh questee sold*ee*...
into Austrian schillings	**in scellini austriaci**
	in shel-l*ee*nee ah-*oo*str*ee*-achee
into French francs	**in franchi francesi**
	in fr*a*nkee franch*ez*-*ee*
into Italian lira	**in lire italiane**
	in l*ee*reh italian-eh
into Swiss francs	**in franchi svizzeri**
	in fr*a*nkee zv*ee*t-tzer*ee*
What's the rate of exchange?	**Qual'è il cambio oggi?**
	qual*eh* il c*a*mbeeo *o*d-j*ee*

LIKELY REACTIONS

Passport, please	**Il passaporto, per favore**
	il pas-saporto pair fav-*oreh*
Sign here	**Firmi qui**
	f*ee*rmee qu*ee*

Your banker's card, please	**La sua carta assegni. per favore**
	la soo-ah carta as-sen-yee pair fav-oreh
Go to the cash desk	**Si accomodi alla cassa**
	see ac-comodee al-la cas-sa

Car travel

ESSENTIAL INFORMATION

- Finding a filling station or garage, see p. 21.
- Is it a self-service station? Look out for **SELF SERVICE.**
- Grades of gasoline:
  BENZINA NORMALE   (2 star, standard)
  BENZINA SUPER   (3 star and above, premium)
  GASOLIO   (diesel)
- 1 gallon is about 4½ litres (accurate enough up to 6 gallons).
- for car repairs, look for:
  AUTORIPARAZIONI   (repairs)
  AUTORIMESSA   (garage)
  MECCANICO   (mechanic)
  ELETTRAUTO   (for electrical bre)
  CARROZZERIA   (for bodywork)
- Petrol stations are usually closed from 12 to 3, and very few offer a 24 hour service (except on motorways).
- In case of a breakdown or an emergency look for the **ACI** (Italian Automobile Club) sign, or dial 116 from any telephone box.
- Unfamiliar road signs and warnings, see p. 123.

WHAT TO SAY

[For numbers see p. 128.]

(Nine) litres of . . .	**(Nove) litri di . . .**
	(nov-eh) leetree dee . . .
(2000) lira of . . .	**(Duemila) lire di . . .**
	(dooeh meela) leereh dee . . .
standard/premium/diesel	**normale/super/gasolio**
	normal-eh/sooper/gazol-yo
Full, please	**Pieno, per favore**
	pee-ehno, pair fav-oreh

Will you check . . .	**Può controllare . . .** poo-*o* control-l*a*r-eh . . .
the oil?	**l'olio?** l*o*l-yo
the battery?	**la batteria?** la bat-ter*e*e-ah
the radiator?	**il radiatore?** il rad-yat*o*reh
the tyres?	**le gomme?** leh g*o*m-meh
I've run out of petrol	**Sono rimasta senza benzina** s*o*nno reem*a*s-ta s*e*ntza bendz*e*ena
Can I borrow a can, please?	**Posso prendere a prestito una latta, per favore?** pos-so prend*e*reh ah prest*e*eto oona l*a*t-ta pair fav-*o*reh
My car has broken down	**La mia macchina s'è rotta** la m*e*e-ah m*a*c-keena seh r*o*t-ta
My car won't start	**La mia macchina non parte** la m*e*e-ah m*a*c-keena non p*a*rteh
I've had an accident	**Ho avuto un incidente** o av*oo*to oon incheed*e*nteh
I've lost my car keys	**Ho perso le chiavi della macchina** o p*a*irso leh kee-*a*h-vee del-la m*a*c-keena
My car is . . .	**La mia macchina è . . .** la m*e*e-ah m*a*c-keena eh . . .
two kilometres away	**a due chilometri** ah d*oo*eh keelom*e*tree
three kilometres away	**a tre chilometri** ah treh keelom*e*tree
Can you help me, please?	**Mi può aiutare, per favore?** mee poo-*o* ayoot*a*r-eh pair fav-*o*reh
Do you do repairs?	**Ripara le macchine?** reep*a*r-ah leh m*a*c-keeneh
I have a puncture	**Ho una gomma a terra** o oona g*o*m-ma ah terra
I have a broken windscreen	**Ho rotto il parabrezza** o r*o*t-to il parabr*e*t-tza
I think the problem is here . . . (*point*)	**Penso che il guasto sia qui . . .** penso keh il goo-*a*sto see-ah quee . . .

1	windscreen wipers	**tergicristalli**
		tairjee-cristal-lee
2	**fuses**	**fusibili**
		foozeebeelee
3	heater	**riscaldamento**
		reescaldamento
4	battery	**batteria**
		bat-teree-ah
5	engine	**motore**
		motoreh
6	fuel pump	**pompa benzina**
		pompa bendzeena
7	starter motor	**motorino d'avviamento**
		motoreeno dav-vee-amento
8	carburettor	**carburatore**
		carboorat-oreh
9	lights	**luci**
		loochee
10	radiator	**radiatore**
		rad-yat-oreh
11	fan belt	**cinghia del ventilatore**
		chinghee-ah del ventilat-oreh
12	generator	**dinamo**
		deenam-o
13	brakes	**freni**
		frehnee
14	clutch	**frizione**
		freetzioneh
15	gear box	**cambio**
		cambeeo
16	steering	**sterzo**
		stairtzo
17	ignition	**accensione**
		at-chensioneh
18	transmission	**trasmissione**
		trasmis-sioneh
19	exhaust	**scappamento**
		scap-pamento
20	indicators	**lampeggiatori**
		lampej-jat-oree

I don't know what's wrong	Non so cosa non va
	non so *coza* non va
Can you ...	Può ...
	poo-*o* ...
repair the fault?	riparare il guasto?
	reepar*ar*-eh il goo-*a*sto
come and look?	venire a vedere?
	ven*eer*eh a ved-*air*eh
estimate the cost?	farmi un preventivo?
	*far*mee oon prevent*ee*vo
write it down?	scriverlo?
	*scree*verlo
Do you accept these coupons?	Accetta questi buoni?
	at-*chet*-ta qu*ee*stee boo-*onee*
How long will the repair take?	Quanto ci vorrà per ripararlo?
	qu*an*to chee vorr*a* pair reeparar-*lo*
When will the car be ready?	Quando sarà pronta la macchina?
	qu*an*do sar*a* pronta la m*a*c-keena
Can I see the bill?	Posso vedere il conto?
	p*os*-so ved-*air*eh il conto
This is my insurance document	Questa è l'assicurazione
	questa eh las-sicooratzioneh

HIRING A CAR

Can I hire a car?	Potrei noleggiare una macchina?
	potr*ay* noled-jar-eh oona m*a*c-keena
I need a car ...	Ho bisogno di una macchina ...
	o beeson-yo dee oona m*a*c-keena ...
for two people	per due persone
	pair d*oo*eh pairs*o*neh
for five people	per cinque persone
	pair ch*in*queh pairs*o*neh
for one day	per un giorno
	pair oon jorno
for five days	per cinque giorni
	pair ch*in*queh jorn*ee*
for a week	per una settimana
	pair oona set-tim*an*-ah

Can you write down ...
Può scrivermi ...
poo-*o* screevermee ...

the deposit to pay?
quant'è il deposito da pagare?
quanteh il dep*oz*-eeto da pag*ar*-eh

the charge per kilometre?
quanto costa al chilometro?
qu*an*to costa al keel*o*metro

the daily charge?
quanto costa al giorno?
qu*an*to costa al jorno

the cost of insurance?
il costo dell'assicurazione?
il *cos*to del-las-sicooratzioneh

Can I leave it in (Turin)?
Posso lasciarla a (Torino)?
pos-so lash*ar*la ah (tor*ee*no)

What documents do I need?
Quali documenti ci vogliono?
qu*al*-ee docoom*e*ntee chee v*o*l-yono

LIKELY REACTIONS

I don't do repairs
Non riparo auto
non reep*ar*-o *ah*-ooto

Where's your car?
Dov'è la sua macchina?
dov-*eh* la soo-ah m*ac*-keena

What make is it?
Che tipo di macchina è?
keh t*ee*po dee m*ac*-keena **eh**

Come back tomorrow/on Monday
Ritorni domani/lunedì
reet*or*nee dom*an*-ee/loon-ed*es*
[*For days of the week see p. 132.*]

We don't hire cars
Non noleggiamo macchine
non noled-j*amo* m*ac*-keeneh

Your driving licence, please
La patente, per favore
la pat*en*teh, pair fav-*or*eh

The mileage is unlimited
Il chilometraggio è illimitato
il keelometr*ad*-jo *eh* il-limit*at*-o

Public transport

ESSENTIAL INFORMATION

- Finding the way to the bus station, a bus stop, a tram stop, the railway station and a taxi rank, see p. 18.
- Remember that queuing for buses is unheard of!
- Taxis can be found at taxi ranks in the main areas of a town, especially at the railway station.
- These are the different types of trains, graded according to speed (slowest to fastest):

  LOCALE
  DIRETTO
  ESPRESSO
  RAPIDO (sometimes first-class only, with supplement to be paid and seats to be reserved – especially on luxury high-speed trains)

- Key words on signs [see also p. 123]:

BIGLIETTI	(tickets)
BINARIO	(platform)
DEPOSITO BAGAGLI	(left luggage)
ENTRATA	(entrance)
FERMATA AUTOBUS	(bus stop)
FS, FERROVIE DELLO STATO	(Italian railways)
INFORMAZIONI	(information)
ORARIO	(timetable)
PROIBITO-VIETATO	(forbidden)
SALITA	(entrance for buses and tram)
USCITA	(exit)

- In the main cities automatic ticket systems are in operation on buses trams and the underground. Tickets must then be bought in advance from bars and tobacconists. Ask for details at the local tourist information offices [see p. 24].

WHAT TO SAY

Where does the train for (Rome) leave from?	Da dove parte il treno per (Roma)?
	da dov-eh parteh il tren-o pair (roma)
At what time does the train leave for (Rome)?	A che ora parte il treno per (Roma)?
	ah keh ora parteh il tren-o pair (roma)
At what time does the train arrive in (Rome)?	A che ora arriva il treno a (Roma)?
	ah keh ora arreeva il tren-o ah (roma)
Is this the train for (Rome)?	È questo il treno per (Roma)?
	eh questo il tren-o pair (roma)
Where does the bus for (Florence) leave from?	Da dove parte l'autobus per (Firenze)?
	da dov-ch parteh la-ootoboos pair (feerentzeh)
At what time does the bus leave for (Florence)?	A che ora parte l'autobus per (Firenze)?
	ah keh ora parteh la-ootoboos pair (feerentzeh)
At what times does the bus arrive in (Florence)?	A che ora arriva l'autobus a (Firenze)?
	ah keh ora arreeva la-ootoboos ah (feerentzeh)
Is this the bus for (Florence)?	È questo l'autobus per (Firenze)?
	eh questo la-ootoboos pair (feerentzeh)
Do I have to change?	Devo cambiare?
	dev-o cambee-ar-eh
Where does ... leave from?	Da dove parte ... ?
	da doveh parteh ...
the bus	l'autobus
	la-ootoboos
the train	il treno
	il tren-o
the underground	la metropolitana
	la metropolitan-a

Where does . . . leave from?	**Da dove parte . . . ?**
	da doveh parteh . . .
the boat/ferry	**il vaporetto/il traghetto**
	il vap-oret-to/il trah-ghet-to
for the airport	**per l'aeroporto**
	pair la-airoporto
for the cathedral	**per la cattedrale**
	pair la cat-tedral-eh
for the beach	**per la spiaggia**
	pair la spee-ad-ja
for the market place	**per il mercato**
	pair il maircat-o
for the railway station	**per la stazione**
	pair la statzioneh
for the town centre	**per il centro città**
	pair il chentro chit-ta
for the town hall	**per il municipio**
	pair il moonicheepio
for St John's church	**per la chiesa di S. Giovanni**
	pair la kee-ehza dee san jovan-nee
for the swimming pool	**per la piscina**
	pair la pisheena
Is this . . .	**È questo . . .**
	eh questo . . .
the bus for the market place?	**l'autobus per il mercato?**
	la-ootobus pair il maircat-o
the tram for the station?	**il tram per la stazione?**
	il tram pair la statzioneh
Where can I get a taxi?	**Dove posso trovare un taxi?**
	dov-eh pos-so trovar-eh oon taxi
Can you put me off at the right stop, please?	**Può farmi scendere alla fermata giusta, per favore?**
	poo-o farmee shendereh al-la fairmat-ah joosta pair fav-oreh
Can I book a seat?	**Posso prenotare un posto?**
	pos-so prenotar-eh oon posto
A single	**Solo andata**
	solo andat-ah
A return	**Andata e ritorno**
	andat-ah eh reetorno
First class	**Prima classe**
	preema clas-seh

Second class	**Seconda classe** seconda clas-seh
One adult	**Un adulto** oon adoolto
Two adults	**Due adulti** dooeh adooltee
and one child	**e un bambino** eh oon bambeeno
and two children	**e due bambini** eh dooeh bambeenee
How much is it?	**Quanto costa?** quanto costa

LIKELY REACTIONS

Over there	**Di là** dee la
Here	**Qui** quee
Platform (1)	**Binario (uno)** beenar-eeo (oono)
At (four o'clock)	**Alle (quattro)** al-leh (quat-tro)
[For times see p. 130.]	
Change at (Milan)	**Cambi a (Milano)** cambee ah (meelan-o)
Change at (the town hall)	**Cambi al (municipio)** cambee al (moonicheepio)
This is your stop	**Questa è la sua fermata** questa eh la soo-ah fairmat-ah
There's only first class	**C'è solo la prima classe** cheh solo la preema clas-seh
There's a supplement	**C'è un supplemento** cheh oon soop-plemento

Leisure

ESSENTIAL INFORMATION

● Finding the way to a place of entertainment, see p. 18.
● For times of day, see p. 130.
● Important signs, see p. 123.
● In the more popular seaside resorts you have to pay to go on the beach and to hire deckchairs and sunshades.
● Smoking is forbidden in cinemas and theatres, unless specified.
● You should tip theatre usherettes.

WHAT TO SAY

At what time does . . . open?	A che ora apre . . . ? ah keh ora *a*preh . . .
the art gallery	la galleria d'arte la gal-ler*ee*-ah d*a*rteh
the botanical garden	il giardino botanico il jard*ee*no bot*a*n-eeco
the cinema	il cinema il ch*ee*nema
the concert hall	l'auditorium la-ooditor*ee*-oom
the disco	la discoteca la discot*e*c-ah
the museum	il museo il mooz*ai*-o
the night club	il night il night
the sports stadium	lo stadio lo st*a*d-eeo
the swimming pool	la piscina la pish*ee*na
the theatre	il teatro il teh-*a*tro
the zoo	lo zoo lo dzor
At what time does . . . close?	A che ora chiude . . . ? ah keh ora kee-*oo*deh . . .

the art gallery	la galleria d'arte
	la gal-leree-ah darteh
[see above list]	
At what time does . . . start?	A che ora inizia . . .?
	ah keh ora eeneetzia . . .
the cabaret	il cabaret
	il cabareh
the concert	il concerto
	il conchairto
the film	il film
	il feelm
the match	l'incontro
	leencontro
the play	la commedia
	la com-meh-dia
the race	la gara
	la gar-ah
How much is it . . .	Quanto costa . . .
	quanto costa . . .
for an adult?	per un adulto?
	pair oon adoolto
for a child?	per un bambino?
	pair oon bambeeno
Two adults, please	Due adulti, per favore
	dooeh adooltee pair fav-oreh
Three children, please	Tre bambini, per favore
	treh bambeenee pair fav-oreh
[state price, if there is a choice]	
Stalls/circle	Platea/galleria
	plateh-ah/gal-leree-ah
Do you have . . .	Avete . . .
	avet-eh . . .
a programme?	un programma?
	oon program-ma
a guide book?	una guida?
	oona goo-eeda
Where's the toilet, please?	Dov'è il bagno, per favore?
	dov-eh il ban-yo pair fav-oreh
Where's the cloakroom?	Dov'è il guardaroba?
	dov-eh il gwardaroba

I would like lessons in ...	Vorrei delle lezioni ... vorr*ay* del-leh letzion*ee* ...
skiing	di sci dee sh*ee*
sailing	di vela dee v*eh*-la
water skiing	di sci d'acqua dee shee d*a*cqua
sub-aqua diving	di nuoto sub dee nw*o*to s*oo*b
Can I hire ...	Potrei noleggiare ... potr*ay* noled-j*ar*-eh ...
some skis?	degli sci? del-yee sh*ee*
some ski-boots?	degli scarponi da sci? del-yee scarpon*ee* da sh*ee*
a boat?	una barca? oona b*a*rca
a fishing rod?	una canna da pesca? oona c*a*n-na da p*e*sca
a deck chair?	una sedia a sdraio? oona sed-ee-ah ah zdr*a*-yo
a sun umbrella?	un ombrellone? oon ombrel-l*o*neh
the necessary equipment?	l'equipaggiamento necessario? lequeepad-jamento neches-s*ar*-eeo
How much is it ...	Quanto costa ... qu*a*nto c*o*sta ...
per day/per hour?	al giorno/all'ora? al j*o*rno/al-l*o*ra
Do I need a licence?	Devo avere un'autorizzazione? d*e*v-o av*ai*reh oon ah-ootorit-tzat-zion*eh*

Asking if things are allowed

ESSENTIAL INFORMATION

- May one smoke here?
  May we smoke here?
  May I smoke here?
  Can one smoke here?
  Can we smoke here?
  Is it possible to smoke here?

  Si può fumare qui?

- All these English variations can be expressed in *one* way in Italian. To save space, only the first English version (May one ... ?) is shown below.

WHAT TO SAY

Excuse me, please	Mi scusi, per favore
	mee sc*oo*zee pair fav-*o*reh
May one ...	Si può ...
	see poo-*o* ...
camp here?	campeggiare qui?
	camped-j*a*r-eh quee
come in?	entrare?
	entr*a*r-eh
dance here?	ballare qui?
	bal-l*a*r-eh quee
fish here?	pescare qui?
	pesc*a*r-eh quee
get a drink here?	avere qualcosa da bere qui?
	av*ai*reh qualc*o*za da b*ai*reh quee
get out this way?	uscire di qui?
	oosh*ee*reh dee quee
get something to eat here?	mangiare qualcosa qui?
	man-j*a*r-eh qualc*o*za quee
leave one's things here?	lasciare della roba qui?
	lash*a*r-eh del-la r*o*ba quee
look around?	guardare in giro?
	goo-ard*a*r-eh in j*ee*ro
park here?	parcheggiare qui?
	parked-j*a*r-eh quee

May one ...	**Si può ...**
	see poo-*o* ...
picnic here?	**fare un picnic qui?**
	f*a*r-eh oon pic*ni*c quee
sit here?	**sedere qui?**
	sed*ai*reh quee
smoke here?	**fumare qui?**
	foom*a*r-eh quee
swim here?	**nuotare qui?**
	nwot*a*r-eh quee
take photos here?	**prendere una foto qui?**
	prend*e*reh oona foto quee
telephone here?	**telefonare qui?**
	telefon*a*r-eh quee
wait here?	**aspettare qui?**
	aspet-t*a*r-eh quee

LIKELY REACTIONS

Yes, certainly	**Sì, certo**
	see ch*a*irto
Help yourself	**Si serva**
	see s*ai*rva
I think so	**Penso di sì**
	p*e*nso dee s*ee*
Of course	**Naturalmente**
	natooralmenteh
Yes, but be careful	**Sì, ma faccia attenzione**
	see ma f*a*t-cha at-tentzioneh
No, certainly not	**Certamente no**
	ch*ai*rtamenteh n*o*h
I don't think so	**Credo di no**
	cred-o dee n*o*h
Not normally	**Normalmente no**
	normalmenteh n*o*h
Sorry	**Mi dispiace**
	mee dispi-*a*h-cheh

Reference

PUBLIC NOTICES

● Key words on signs for drivers, pedestrians, travellers, shoppers and overnight guests.

ACCENDERE I FARI	Lights on
ACQUA POTABILE	Drinking water
AFFITTANSI	For rent
ALT	Halt
APERTO	Open
ARRIVI	Arrivals
ASCENSORE	Lift
ASPETTARE	Wait
ATTENTI AL CANE	Beware of the dog
ATTENZIONE	Look out, beware
AUTOCARRI	Lorries, heavy vehicles
AUTO LAVAGGIO	Car wash
AUTOSTRADA (A PAGAMENTO)	Motorway (with toll)
AVANTI	Go
BAGNO	WC, bathroom
BIGLIETTERIA (A TERRA)	Ticket office (not on the bus)
BIGLIETTI	Tickets
BINARIO	Platform
CADUTA MASSI	Falling stones
CALDO (C)	Hot (tap) (H)
CAMERE LIBERE	Rooms to rent
CARABINIERI	Police
CASSA	Cash desk
CHIUSO	Closed
CHIUSO PER FERIE	Closed for holidays
CHIUSO PER TURNO	Closed on shift basis
CON PIOGGIA, GELO, NEVE	In rain, ice, snow, (slippery road)
DA AFFITTARE	For rent
DEPOSITO BAGAGLI	Left luggage
DEVIAZIONE	Detour
DISPORSI SU UNA FILA	Single lane traffic
DIVIETO	Forbidden

DIVIETO DI PESCA	Fishing forbidden
DIVIETO DI SOSTA	No parking
DIVIETO DI TRANSITO	No through road
DOCCIA	Shower
DOGANA	Customs
DOMANI	Tomorrow
ECCETTO (AUTOBUS)	Except (buses)
ENTRATA	Entrance
ENTRATA LIBERA	Entrance free
FINE AUTOSTRADA	End of motorway
FERMATA (A RICHIESTA)	(Request) stop
FREDDO (F)	Cold (tap) (C)
FUMATORI	Smokers
GABINETTO	WC
GRATUITO	Free
GUIDA	Guide
GUIDARE LENTAMENTE	Drive slowly
INCROCIO	Crossroads
INGRESSO (LIBERO)	Entrance (free)
INIZIO AUTOSTRADA	Beginning of motorway
I TRASGRESSORI SARANNO PUNITI	Trespassers will be prosecuted
LAVORI IN CORSO	Construction
LIBERO	Free
LIMITE DI VELOCITÀ	Speed limit
LISTINO PREZZI	Price list
METROPOLITANA	Underground
MONETA	Coins
NON POTABILE	Not for drinking
NON TOCCARE	Do not touch
OBBLIGATORIO L'USO DELLE CATENE	Snow chains obligatory
OCCUPATO	Engaged
OFFERTA SPECIALE	Special offer
OGGI	Today
PAGAMENTO	Payment
PARCHEGGIO	Parking
PARCHEGGIO LIMITATO	Restricted parking
PARTENZE	Departures
PASSAGGIO A LIVELLO	Level crossing
PEDAGGIO	Toll
PEDONI	Pedestrians

PERICOLO	Danger
PIANO (PRIMO, SECONDO, TERZO, TERRA, SEMINTERRATO)	Floor (first, second, third, ground, basement)
POLIZIA	Police
PORTINAIO	Caretaker
PRECEDENZA	Priority
PRECEDENZA ALLA DESTRA	Priority to the right
PRENOTAZIONI	Reservations
PRONTO SOCCORSO	First aid
RALLENTARE	Slow down
RISERVATO	Reserved
SALA D'ATTESA	Waiting room
SALDI	Sales
SCALA MOBILE	Escalator
SCUOLA	School
SENSO UNICO	One way (street)
SENSO VIETATO	No entry
SERVIZI	WC
SIGNORE	Ladies
SIGNORI	Gentlemen
SILENZIO	Silence
SOSTA AUTORIZZATA (DALLE . . .)	Parking allowed (certain times)
SOSTA VIETATA	No parking
SOTTOPASSAGGIO	Subway
SPINGERE	Push
STRADA CHIUSA	Road closed
STRADA GUASTA	Road up
STRADA PERICOLOSA	Dangerous road
STRADA RISTRETTA	Road narrows
SUONARE IL CAMPANELLO	Ring the bell
SUONARE IN PORTINERIA	Ring the caretaker
SVOLTA	Bend
TENERE LA DESTRA	Keep right
TIRARE	Pull
TOELETTA	WC
UFFICIO INFORMAZIONI	Information office
USCITA	Exit

USCITA AUTOSTRADA	Motorway exit
USCITA D'EMERGENZA	Emergency exit
VAGONE RISTORANTE	Dining car
VALANGHE	Avalanches
VICOLO CIECO	Cul-de-sac
VIETATO	Forbidden
VIETATO FUMARE	No smoking
VIETATO IL SORPASSO	Passing forbidden
VIETATO INTRODURRE CANI	No dogs allowed
VIETATO L'INGRESSO (VEICOLI)	No entry (for vehicles)
VIETATO IL TRANSITO	No through road
VIETATO TRANSITO AUTOCARRI	No through road for lorries
ZONA DISCO	Parking disc required
ZONA PEDONALE	Pedestrian area
ZONA SLAVINE	Avalanche area

ABBREVIATIONS

ACI	Automobile Club d'Italia	Italian Automobile Club
AGIP	Azienda Generale Italiana Petroli	chain of petrol stations
alb	albergo	hotel
alt	altezza	height
ANAS	Azienda Nazionale Autonoma delle Strade Statali	State Highway Authority
avv	avvocato	solicitor
CIT	Compagnia Italiana Turismo	Italian Travel Agency
cm	corrente mese	instant
CRI	Croce Rossa Italiana	Italian Red Cross
dc	dopo Cristo	after Christ (AD)
dott	dottore	doctor (medical and university graduate)
EA	Ente Autonomo	Authority
EI	Esercito Italiano	Italian Army
ENIT	Ente Nazionale Italiano Turismo	Italian State Tourist Authority
fatt	fattura	invoice

ferr	ferrovia	railway
FS	Ferrovie dello Stato	State Railways
GdF	Guardie di Finanza	customs officers
h	ora	hour
ht	ettogrammo	100 grams
ing	ingegnere	engineer
INAM	Istituto Nazionale Assicurazione Malattie	National (Medical) Insurance
IVA	Imposta Valore Aggiunto	VAT
L it	Lire Italiane	Italian lira
L st	Lire Sterline	£ Sterling
naz	nazionale	national
PP TT	Poste Telecomunicazioni	post office
PS	Pubblica Sicurezza	police
PT	Poste Telegrafi	post office
racc	raccomandata	registered letter
RAI	Radio Audizione Italiana	Italian Broadcasting Company
sig	signore	Mr
sigra	signora	Mrs
signa	signorina	Miss
SpA	Società per Azioni	Limited Company
succ	succursale	branch
tel	telefono	telephone
vle	viale	boulevard
VU	Vigile Urbano	traffic police

NUMBERS

Cardinal numbers

0	**zero**	dza*i*ro
1	**uno**	*oo*no
2	**due**	d*oo*eh
3	**tre**	treh
4	**quattro**	qu*aa*t-tro
5	**cinque**	ch*i*nqueh
6	**sei**	say
7	**sette**	s*e*t-teh
8	**otto**	*o*t-to
9	**nove**	noveh
10	**dieci**	dee-*e*chee
11	**undici**	*oo*ndeechee
12	**dodici**	dodeechee
13	**tredici**	trehdeechee
14	**quattordici**	quat-tordeechee
15	**quindici**	qu*i*ndeechee
16	**sedici**	sehdeechee
17	**diciassette**	deechas-s*e*t-teh
18	**diciotto**	deech*o*t-to
19	**diciannove**	deechan-noveh
20	**venti**	ventee
21	**ventuno**	ven-t*oo*no
22	**ventidue**	ventee-d*oo*eh
23	**ventitré**	ventee-treh
24	**ventiquattro**	ventee-qu*a*t-tro
25	**venticinque**	ventee-ch*i*nqueh
26	**ventisei**	ventee-s*a*y
27	**ventisette**	ventee-s*e*t-teh
28	**ventotto**	vent*o*t-to
29	**ventinove**	ventee-noveh
30	**trenta**	trenta

For numbers beyond 20 follow the pattern of **venti**: *keep the final vowel except with one and eight.*

31	**trentuno**	tren-t*oo*no
35	**trentacinque**	trenta-ch*i*nqueh
38	**trentotto**	trent*o*t-to
40	**quaranta**	quar*a*nta

41	quarantuno	quarant-*oono*
45	quarantacinque	quaranta-ch*i*nqueh
48	quarantotto	quarant*o*t-to
50	cinquanta	chinqu*a*nta
55	cinquantacinque	chinquanta-ch*i*nqueh
60	sessanta	ses-s*a*nta
65	sessantacinque	ses-santa-ch*i*nqueh
70	settanta	set-t*a*nta
80	ottanta	ot-t*a*nta
90	novanta	nov*a*nta
100	cento	chento
101	centouno	chento-*oono*
102	centodue	chento-d*oo*eh
125	centoventicinque	chentoventee-ch*i*nqueh
150	centocinquanta	chento-chin-qu*a*nta
175	centosettantacinque	chentoset-tanta-ch*i*nqueh
200	duecento	d*oo*eh-chento
300	trecento	treh-chento
400	quattrocento	quat-tro-chento
500	cinquecento	chinqueh-chento
1000	mille	m*ee*l-leh
1500	millecinquecento	m*ee*l-leh-chinqueh-chento
2000	duemila	d*oo*eh-m*ee*la
5000	cinquemila	chinqueh-m*ee*la
10,000	diecimila	dee-echee-m*ee*la
100,000	centomila	chento-m*ee*la
1,000,000	un milione	*oo*n meel-yoneh

Ordinal numbers

1st	primo (1°)	pr*ee*mo
2nd	secondo (2°)	secondo
3rd	terzo (3°)	t*ai*rtzo
4th	quarto (4°)	qu*a*rto
5th	quinto (5°)	qu*ee*nto
6th	sesto (6°)	sesto
7th	settimo (7°)	set-t*ee*mo
8th	ottavo (8°)	ot-t*a*vo
9th	nono (9°)	no-no
10th	decimo (10°)	d*e*cheemo
11th	undicesimo (11°)	oond*ee*cheh-zeemo
12th	dodicesimo (12°)	dod*ee*cheh-zeemo

TIME

What time is it?	**Che ora è?**
	keh ora *eh*
It's one o'clock	**È l'una**
	eh l*oo*na
It's ...	**Sono ...**
	so*nn*o ...
two o'clock	**le due**
	leh d*oo*eh
three o'clock	**le tre**
	leh tr*eh*
four o'clock	**le quattro**
	leh qu*a*t-tro
in the morning	**di mattino**
	dee mat-*tee*no
in the afternoon	**di pomeriggio**
	dee pomair*eed*-jo
in the evening	**di sera**
	dee s*ai*ra
in the night	**di notte**
	dee n*o*t-teh
It's ...	**È ...**
	eh ...
noon	**mezzogiorno**
	med-dzoj*o*rno
midnight	**mezzanotte**
	med-dzan*o*t-teh
It's ...	**Sono ...**
	so*nn*o ...
five past five	**le cinque e cinque**
	leh ch*i*nqueh eh ch*i*nqueh
ten past five	**le cinque e dieci**
	leh ch*i*nqueh eh dee-*e*chee
a quarter past five	**le cinque e un quarto**
	leh ch*i*nqueh eh oon qu*aa*rto
twenty past five	**le cinque e venti**
	leh ch*i*nqueh eh v*e*ntee
twenty-five past five	**le cinque e venticinque**
	leh ch*i*nqueh eh ventee-ch*i*nqueh
half past five	**le cinque e mezza**
	leh ch*i*nqueh eh m*e*d-dza
twenty-five to six	**le sei meno venticinque**
	leh say men-o ventee-ch*i*nqueh

twenty to six	le sei meno venti
	leh say men-o ventee
a quarter to six	le sei meno un quarto
	leh say men-o oon quaarto
ten to six	le sei meno dieci
	leh say men-o dee-echee
five to six	le sei meno cinque
	leh say men-o chinqueh
At what time . . . (does the train leave)?	A che ora (parte il treno)?
	ah keh ora parteh il tren-o
At . . .	Alle . . .
	al-leh . . .
13.00	tredici
	treh-deechee
14.05	quattordici e cinque
	quat-tordeechee eh chinqueh
15.10	quindici e dieci
	quin-deechee eh dee-echee
16.15	sedici e quindici
	seh-deechee eh quin-deechee
17.20	diciassette e venti
	deechas-set-teh eh ventee
18.25	diciotto e venticinque
	deechot-to eh ventee-chinqueh
19.30	diciannove e trenta
	dichan-noveh eh trenta
20.35	venti e trentacinque
	ventee eh trenta-chinqueh
21.40	ventuno e quaranta
	vent-oono eh quaranta
22.45	ventidue e quarantacinque
	ventee-dooeh eh quaranta-chinqueh
23.50	ventitrè e cinquanta
	ventee-treh eh chinquanta
0.55	zero e cinquantacinque
	dzairo eh chinquanta-chinqueh
in ten minutes	fra dieci minuti
	fra dee-echee meenootee
in a quarter of an hour	fra un quarto d'ora
	fra oon quaarto dora
in half an hour	fra mezz'ora
	fra med-dzora
in three-quarters of an hour	fra tre quarti d'ora
	fra treh quaartee dora

DAYS

Monday	**lunedí** loon-ed*ee*
Tuesday	**martedí** mart-ed*ee*
Wednesday	**mercoledí** maircol-ed*ee*
Thursday	**giovedí** jov-ed*ee*
Friday	**venerdí** venaird*ee*
Saturday	**sabato** s*a*bato
Sunday	**domenica** dom*e*n-eeca
last Monday	**lunedí scorso** loon-ed*ee* sc*o*rso
next Tuesday	**martedí prossimo** mart-ed*ee* pros-seemo
on Wednesday	**mercoledí** maircol-ed*ee*
on Thursdays	**al giovedí** al jov-ed*ee*
until Friday	**fino a venerdí** f*ee*no ah venaird*ee*
before Saturday	**prima di sabato** pr*ee*ma dee s*a*bato
after Sunday	**dopo domenica** d*o*p-o dom*e*n-eeca
the day before yesterday	**l'altro ieri** l*a*ltro y*a*ir*ee*
two days ago	**due giorni fa** d*oo*eh j*o*rnee f*a*
yesterday	**ieri** y*a*ir*ee*
yesterday morning	**ieri mattina** y*a*ir*ee* mat-t*ee*na
yesterday afternoon	**ieri pomeriggio** y*a*ir*ee* pomair*ee*d-jo
last night	**ieri sera** y*a*ir*ee* s*e*h-ra

today	**oggi**
	*o*d-jee
this morning	**questa mattina**
	qu*e*sta mat-*tee*na
this afternoon	**questo pomeriggio**
	qu*e*sto pomair*ee*d-jo
tonight	**questa ser*a***
	qu*e*sta s*e*h-ra
tomorrow	**domani**
	dom*a*n-ee
tomorrow morning	**domani mattina**
	dom*a*n-ee mat-*tee*na
tomorrow afternoon	**domani pomeriggio**
	dom*a*n-ee pomair*ee*d-jo
tomorrow evening ⎤	**domani sera**
tomorrow night ⎦	dom*a*n-ee s*e*h-ra
the day after tomorrow	**dopo domani**
	d*o*p-o dom*a*n-ee

MONTHS AND DATES

January	**gennaio**
	jen-n*a*h-yo
February	**febbraio**
	feb-br*a*h-yo
March	**marzo**
	m*a*rtzo
April	**aprile**
	apr*ee*leh
May	**maggio**
	m*a*d-jo
June	**giugno**
	j*oo*n-yo
July	**luglio**
	l*oo*l-yo
August	**agosto**
	ag*o*sto
September	**settembre**
	set-t*e*mbreh
October	**ottobre**
	ot-t*o*breh

November	**novembre**
	novembreh
December	**dicembre**
	deechembreh
in January	**in gennaio**
	in jen-nah-yo
until February	**fino a febbraio**
	feeno ah feb-brah-yo
before March	**prima di marzo**
	preema dee martzo
after April	**dopo aprile**
	dopo apreeleh
during May	**durante maggio**
	dooranteh mad-jo
not until June	**non fino a giugno**
	non feeno ah joon-yo
the beginning of July	**l'inizio di luglio**
	lineetzio dee lool-yo
the middle of August	**la metà di agosto**
	la meta dee agosto
the end of September	**la fine di settembre**
	la feeneh dee set-tembreh
last month	**il mese scorso**
	il mez-eh scorso
this month	**questo mese**
	questo mez-eh
next month	**il mese prossimo**
	il mez-eh pros-seemo
in spring	**in primavera**
	in preemavaira
in summer	**in estate**
	in estat-eh
in autumn	**in autunno**
	in ah-ootoon-no
in winter	**in inverno**
	in invairno
this year	**quest'anno**
	questan-no
last year	**l'anno scorso**
	lan-no scorso
next year	**l'anno prossimo**
	lan-no pros-seemo

in 1982	nel mille novecento ottantadue
	nel m*ee*l-leh noveh-ch*e*nto ot-tanta-d*oo*eh
in 1985	nel mille novecento ottantacinque
	nel m*ee*l-leh noveh-ch*e*nto ot-tanta-ch*i*nqueh
in 1990	nel mille novecento novanta
	nel m*ee*l-leh noveh-ch*e*nto nov*a*nta
What's the date today?	Qual'è la data di oggi?
	qual-*e*h la d*a*t-ah dee *o*d-jee
It's the 6th of March	È il sei di marzo
	eh il say dee m*a*rtzo
It's the 12th of April	È il dodici di aprile
	eh il d*o*deechee dee apr*ee*leh
It's the 21st of August	È il ventuno di agosto
	eh il vent*oo*no dee ag*o*sto

Public holidays

● On these holidays offices, shops and schools are closed.

1 January	**Primo dell'anno**	New Year's Day
	Capodanno	
...	**Lunedí dell'Angelo**	Easter Monday
25 April	**Anniversario della Liberazione**	Liberation Day
1 May	**Festa dei Lavoratori**	Labour Day
15 August	**Assunzione**	Assumption
1 November	**Tutti i Santi**	All Saints Day
	I Morti	
8 December	**Immacolata Concezione**	Immaculate Conception
25 December	**Natale**	Christmas
26 December	**Santo Stefano**	Boxing Day

COUNTRIES AND NATIONALITIES

Countries

Australia	(l') Australia
	(l) a-oostral-ya
Austria	(l') Austria
	(l) a-oostree-ah
Belgium	(il) Belgio
	(il) bel-jo
Britain	(la) Gran Bretagna
	(la) gran bretan-ya
Canada	(il) Canada
	(il) canada
East Africa	(l') Africa Est
	(l) africa aist
Eire	(l') Eire
	(l) eh-eereh
England	(l') Inghilterra
	(l) ing-eeltairra
Greece	(la) Grecia
	(la) graicha
India	(l') India
	(l) india
Italy	(l') Italia
	(l) italia
Luxembourg	(il) Lussemburgo
	(il) loos-semboorgo
Netherlands	(i) Paesi Bassi
	(ee) pah-ehzee bas-see
New Zealand	(la) Nuova Zelanda
	(la) nwova zailanda
Northern Ireland	(l') Irlanda del Nord
	(l) eerlanda del nord
Pakistan	(il) Pakistan
	(il) pakistan
Portugal	(il) Portogallo
	(il) portogal-lo
Scotland	(la) Scozia
	(la) scotzia
Spain	(la) Spagna
	(la) span-ya

Switzerland	(la) Svizzera
	(la) zveet-tzera
United States	(gli) Stati Uniti
	(l-yee) stat-ee ooneetee
Wales	(il) Galles
	(il) gal-les
West Germany	(la) Germania Ovest
	(la) jairman-ya ovaist
West Indies	(le) Indie Occidentali
	(leh) eendi-eh ot-chidental-ee

Nationalities
(Use the first alternative for men, the second for women)

American	americano/americana
	american-o/american-ah
Australian	australiano/australiana
	ah-oostral-yan-o/ah-oostral-yan-ah
Canadian	canadese
	canadaizeh
East African	est africano/est africana
	aist african-o/aist african-ah
English (used for 'British')	inglese
	inglaizeh
Indian	indiano/indiana
	indian-o/indian-ah
Irish	irlandese
	irlandaizeh
a New Zealander	neozelandese
	nai-odzeland-aizeh
a Pakistani	pachistano/pachistana
	pakistan-o/pakistan-ah
Scots	scozzese
	scot-tzaizeh
South African	sudafricano/sudafricana
	soodafrican-o/soodafrican-ah
Welsh	gallese
	gal-laizeh
West Indian	indiano occidentale/
	indiana occidentale
	indian-o ot-chidental-eh/
	indian-ah ot-chidental-eh

DEPARTMENT STORE GUIDE

Abbigliamento e accessori neonato-bambini	Babies–children's department
Abbigliamento e attrezzi sportivi	Sports clothing and equipment
Abbigliamento donna	Ladies' fashions
Abbigliamento uomo	Men's fashions
Accessori auto	Car accessories
Accessori bagno	Bathroom accessories
Alimentari	Food
Arredamento (cucine)	Furniture (kitchen)
Articoli da campeggio	Camping equipment
Articoli casalinghi	Household appliances
Articoli fotografici	Photography
Articoli da fumo	Smokers
Articoli da pesca	Fishing equipment
Articoli da pulizia	Cleaning materials
Articoli da regalo	Gifts
Articoli per ufficio	Office equipment
Articoli da viaggio	Travel articles
Biancheria	Linen
Borse(tte), portafogli	Bags, wallets
Bricolage	Do-it-yourself
Calzature	Shoes
Calze	Stockings/socks
Camicie(tte)	Shirts (blouses)
Cartoleria	Stationery
Cinture	Belts
Coperte	Blankets
Corsetteria	Underwear
Cosmetici	Cosmetics
Cotoni	Cottons
Cravatte	Ties
Cristalleria	Crystal
Dischi	Records
Elettrodomestici	Electrical appliances
Ferramenta	Hardware
Fotocopie	Photocopies
Foulards	Scarves
Giocattoli	Toys
Gioielli	Jewellery

Gonne	Skirts
Guanti	Gloves
Impermeabili	Rainwear
Lana	Wool (knitting)
Libri	Books
Maglieria	Knitwear
Mare	Beach clothes
Maternità	Maternity
Mercerie	Haberdashery
Mobili	Furniture
Moda giovane	Young fashions
Modisteria	Millinery
Ombrelli	Umbrellas
Orologi	Watches
Pantaloni	Trousers
Pellicceria	Furs
Piano	Floor
Porcellane	Porcelain
Primo piano	First floor
Profumeria	Perfumery
Quarto piano	Fourth floor
Radio-televisori	Radios–televisions
Ristorante	Restaurant
Sciarpe	Scarves
Secondo piano	Second floor
Seminterrato	Basement
Tacco espresso-chiavi	Heel bar–keys cut
Taglie forti	Outsize department
Tappeti	Carpets
Tende	Curtains
Terzo piano	Third floor
Tessuti	Fabrics
Ufficio informazioni	Information office
Ufficio vendite a credito	Credit sales department
Ufficio viaggi	Travel agency
Vetro-ceramica	Glass–china

CONVERSION TABLES

Read the centre column of these tables from right to left to convert from metric to imperial and from left to right to convert from imperial to metric e.g. 5 litres = 8.80 pints; 5 pints = 2.84 litres.

pints		litres	gallons		litres
1.76	1	0.57	0.22	1	4.55
3.52	2	1.14	0.44	2	9.09
5.28	3	1.70	0.66	3	13.64
7.07	4	2.27	0.88	4	18.18
8.80	5	2.84	1.00	5	22.73
10.56	6	3.41	1.32	6	27.28
12.32	7	3.98	1.54	7	31.82
14.08	8	4.55	1.76	8	36.37
15.84	9	5.11	1.98	9	40.91

ounces		grams	pounds		kilos
0.04	1	28.35	2.20	1	0.45
0.07	2	56.70	4.41	2	0.91
0.11	3	85.05	6.61	3	1.36
0.14	4	113.40	8.82	4	1.81
0.18	5	141.75	11.02	5	2.27
0.21	6	170.10	13.23	6	2.72
0.25	7	198.45	15.43	7	3.18
0.28	8	226.80	17.64	8	3.63
0.32	9	255.15	19.84	9	4.08

inches		centimetres	yards		metres
0.39	1	2.54	1.09	1	0.91
0.79	2	5.08	2.19	2	1.83
1.18	3	7.62	3.28	3	2.74
1.58	4	10.16	4.37	4	3.66
1.95	5	12.70	5.47	5	4.57
2.36	6	15.24	6.56	6	5.49
2.76	7	17.78	7.66	7	6.40
3.15	8	20.32	8.65	8	7.32
3.54	9	22.86	9.84	9	8.23

miles		kilometres
0.62	1	1.61
1.24	2	3.22
1.86	3	4.83
2.49	4	6.44
3.11	5	8.05
3.73	6	9.66
4.35	7	11.27
4.97	8	12.87
5.59	9	14.48

A quick way to convert kilometres to miles: divide by 8 and multiply by 5. To convert miles to kilometres: divide by 5 and multiply by 8.

fahrenheit ($°F$)	centigrade ($°C$)		lbs/ sq in	k/ sq cm
212°	100°	boiling point	18	1.3
100°	38°		20	1.4
98.4°	36.9°	body temperature	22	1.5
86°	30°		25	1.7
77°	25°		29	2.0
68°	20°		32	2.3
59°	15°		35	2.5
50°	10°		36	2.5
41°	5°		39	2.7
32°	0°	freezing point	40	2.8
14°	–10°		43	3.0
–4°	–20°		45	3.2
			46	3.2
			50	3.5
			60	4.2

To convert $°C$ to $°F$: divide by 5, multiply by 9 and add 32. To convert $°F$ to $°C$: take away 32, divide by 9 and multiply by 5.

CLOTHING SIZES

Remember – always try on clothes before buying. Clothing sizes are usually unreliable.

women's dresses and suits

Europe	38	40	42	44	46	48
UK	32	34	36	38	40	42
USA	10	12	14	16	18	20

men's suits and coats

Europe	46	48	50	52	54	56
UK and USA	36	38	40	42	44	46

men's shirts

Europe	36	37	38	39	41	42	43
UK and USA	14	14½	15	15½	16	16½	17

socks

Europe	38–39	39–40	40–41	41–42	42–43
UK and USA	9½	10	10½	11	11½

shoes

Europe	34	35½	36½	38	39	41	42	43	44	45
UK	2	3	4	5	6	7	8	9	10	11
USA	3½	4½	5½	6½	7½	8½	9½	10½	11½	12½

Do it yourself

Some notes on the language

This section does not deal with 'grammar' as such. The purpose here is to explain some of the most obvious and elementary nuts and bolts of the language, based on the principal phrases included in the book. This information should enable you to produce numerous sentences of your own making.

There is no pronunciation guide in this section, partly because it would get in the way of the explanations and partly because you have to do it yourself at this stage if you are serious – work out the pronunciation from all the earlier examples in the book.

THE

All nouns in Italian belong to one of two genders: masculine or feminine, irrespective of whether they refer to living beings or inanimate objects.

The (singular)	masculine	feminine
the address	l'indirizzo	
the apple		la mela
the bill	il conto	
the cup of tea		la tazza di tè
the glass of wine	il bicchiere di vino	
the key		la chiave
the luggage	(this is only plural in Italian, see below)	
the menu	il menú	
the newspaper	il giornale	
the receipt		la ricevuta
the sandwich	il panino	
the suitcase		la valigia
the telephone directory		la guida telefonica
the timetable	l'orario	
the travel agent's		l'agenzia di viaggi
the zoo	lo zoo	

Important things to remember

- *The* is il before most masculine nouns and la before feminine nouns.
- *The* is lo before certain masculine nouns because of the way they are spelt, notably those which begin with a 'z', e.g. lo zoo.
- *The* is l' before masculine and feminine nouns which begin with a vowel: l'indirizzo (*m*) and l'agenzia di viaggi (*f*).
- You can often predict if a singular noun is masculine or feminine by its ending. Masculine nouns usually end in 'o' and feminine nouns in 'a'. But there are several exceptions, notably a whole group of nouns which end in 'e', e.g. il giornale, so you should learn and remember all genders. If you are reading a word with il, lo or la in front of it, you can detect its gender immediately: il menú and lo zoo are masculine (*m*. in dictionaries) and la valigia is feminine (*f*. in dictionaries).
- Does it matter? Not unless you want to make a serious attempt to speak correctly and scratch beneath the surface of the language. You would be understood if you said la menú or even il agenzia di viaggi, provided your pronunciation was good.

The (plural)	masculine	feminine
the addresses	gli indirizzi	
the apples		le mele
the bills	i conti	
the cups of tea		le tazze di tè
the glasses of wine	i bicchieri di vino	
the keys		le chiavi
the luggage	i bagagli	
the menus	i menú	
the newspapers	i giornali	
the receipts		le ricevute
the sandwiches	i panini	
the suitcases		le valigie
the telephone directories		le guide telefoniche
the timetables	gli orari	
the travel agents		le agenzie di viaggi
the zoos	gli zoo	

Important things to remember

● Most masculine nouns in the plural end in 'i' and most feminine nouns end in 'e'.
● *The* is i before most masculine nouns in the plural. However where in the singular *the* is ' or lo, in the plural *the* is gli. [*See two tables above.*]
● *The* is le before all feminine nouns in the plural.
● In Italian, luggage is always regarded as plural. It is never used to mean a singular item.

Practise saying and writing the following sentences in Italian; note that there are two ways of saying *have you got*, politely, in Italian: ha (when speaking to one person); avete (when speaking to more than one person or in an 'organization', e.g. a hotel, a shop or a tourist information office):

Have you got the key?	Avete la chiave?
Have you got the luggage?	Avete .. ?
Have you got the telephone directory?	Ha ... ?
Have you got the menu?	
I'd like the key	Vorrei la chiave
I'd like the receipt	Vorrei ...
I'd like the bill	
I'd like the keys	
Where is the key?	Dov'è la chiave?
Where is the timetable?	Dov'è ... ?
Where is the address?	
Where is the zoo?	
Where is the suitcase?	
Where is the travel agent's?	
Where are the keys?	Dove sono le chiavi?
Where are the sandwiches?	Dove sono ... ?
Where are the apples?	
Where are the suitcases?	
Where is the luggage?	Dove sono ... ?
Where can I get the key?	Dove posso trovare la chiave?
Where can I get the address?	Dove posso trovare ... ?
Where can I get the timetables?	

Now try to make up more sentences along the same lines. Try adding please: per favore, at the end.

A/AN

A/an (singular)	masculine	feminine
an address	un indirizzo	
an apple		una mela
a bill	un conto	
a cup of tea		una tazza di tè
a glass of wine	un bicchiere di vino	
a key		una chiave
a menu	un menú	
a newspaper	un giornale	
a receipt		una ricevuta
a sandwich	un panino	
a suitcase		una valigia
a telephone directory		una guida telefonica
a timetable	un orario	
a travel agent's		un'agenzia di viaggi
a zoo	uno zoo	

Some/any (plural)	masculine	feminine
addresses	degli indirizzi	
apples		delle mele
bills	dei conti	
cups of tea		della tazze di tè
glasses of wine	dei bicchieri di vino	
keys		delle chiavi
luggage	dei bagagli	
menus	dei menú	
newspapers	dei giornali	
receipts		delle ricevute
sandwiches	dei panini	
suitcases		delle valigie
telephone directories		delle guide telefoniche
timetables	degli orari	
travel agents		delle agenzie di viaggi
zoos	degli zoo	

Important things to remember

● *A* or *an* is un before most masculine nouns and **una** before most feminine nouns.
● Before the group of masculine nouns which start with a **'z'**, *a* or *an* is **uno**.
● Before feminine nouns which begin with a vowel, *a* or *an* is **un'**.
● *Some* or *any* is:
   dei before most masculine nouns in the plural.
   delle before all feminine nouns in the plural.
● Before masculine nouns in the plural which begin with a vowel, **or** the **'z'** group, *some* or *any* is degli.
● In certain expressions in Italian, dei, delle or degli are left out; see an example of this in the sentences marked * below.

Practise saying and writing these sentences in Italian:

Have you got a receipt?	Ha una ricevuta?
Have you got a menu?	Ha . . . ?
I'd like a telephone directory	Vorrei . . .
I'd like some sandwiches	
Where can I get some newspapers?	Dove posso trovare . . . ?
Where can I get a cup of tea?	
Is there a key?	C'è una chiave?
Is there a telephone directory?	C'è . . . ?
Is there a timetable?	
Is there a menu?	
Is there a zoo?	
Is there a travel agent's?	
Are there any keys?	Ci sono delle chiavi?
Are there any newspapers?	Ci sono . . . ?
Are there any sandwiches?	

Now make up more sentences along the same lines.

Then try these new phrases:

Io prendo ... (I'll have ...)
Avrei bisogno di ... (I need .)

I'll have a glass of wine	**Io prendo un bicchiere di vino**
I'll have a cup of tea	**Io prendo ...**
I'll have some sandwiches	
I'll have some apples	
I need a cup of tea	**Avrei bisogno di una tazza di tè**
I need a key	**Avrei bisogno di ...**
*I need some newspapers	**Avrei bisogno di giornali**
*I need some keys	**Avrei bisogno di ...**
*I need some addresses	**Avrei bisogno di ...**
*I need some sandwiches	
*I need some suitcases	

SOME/ANY

In cases where *some* or *any* refer to more than one thing, such as *some/any ice-creams*, *some/any sunglasses* and *some/any bananas*, **dei**, **degli** and **delle** are used as explained earlier:

dei gelati	(some/any ice-creams)
degli occhiali da sole	(some/any sunglasses)
delle banane	(some/any bananas)

As a guide, you can usually *count* the number of containers or whole items.

In cases where *some* refers to part of a whole thing or an indefinite quantity, the words **dei**, **degli** and **delle** cannot be used.
Look at the list below·

the bread	**il pane**	some bread	**del pane**
the flour	**la farina**	some flour	**della farina**
the oil	**l'olio** (*m*)	some oil	**dell'olio**
the sugar	**lo zucchero**	some sugar	**dello zucchero**
the water	**l'acqua** (*f*)	some water	**dell'acqua**
the wine	**il vino**	some wine	**del vino**

Important things to remember

- **del** is used for masculine nouns.
- **delle** is used for feminine nouns.
- **dell'** is used for both masculine and feminine nouns which begin with a vowel.
- **dello** is used for the group of masculine nouns which begin with a 'z'.

Can you complete the list below?

the beer	**la birra**	. . .	some beer
the tea	**il tè**	. . .	some tea
the lemonade	**la limonata**	. . .	some lemonade
the aspirin	**l'aspirina** (*f*)	. . .	some aspirin
the cheese	**il formaggio**	. . .	some cheese
the coffee	**il caffè**	. . .	some coffee

Practise saying and writing these sentences in Italian:

Have you got some coffee?	**Avete del caffè?**
Have you got some flour?	
Have you got some sugar?	
I'd like some aspirin	**Vorrei dell'aspirina**
I'd like some oil	
I'd like some bread	
Is there any lemonade?	**C'è della limonata?**
Is there any water?	
Is there any wine?	
Where can I get some cheese?	**Dove posso trovare del formaggio?**
Where can I get some flour?	
Where can I get some water?	
I'll have some beer	**Io prendo della birra**
I'll have some tea	
I'll have some coffee	

THIS AND THAT

There are two words in Italian: **questo** (this), **quello** (that)

If you don't know the Italian for an object, just point and say:

Vorrei quello	I'd like that
Prendo quello	I'll have that
Avrei bisogno di questo	I need this

HELPING OTHERS

You can help yourself with phrases such as:

I'd like . . . a sandwich	Vorrei . . . un panino
Where can I get . . . a cup of tea?	Dove posso trovare . . . una tazza di tè
I'll have . . . a glass of wine	Io prendo . . . un bicchiere di vino
I need . . . a receipt	Avrei bisogno di . . . una ricevuta

If you come across a compatriot having trouble making himself or herself understood, you should be able to speak to the Italian person on their behalf.

It is not necessary to say the words for *he* (lui), *she* (lei) and *I* (io) in Italian unless you want to emphasize them, e.g. *He'll* have a beer and *I'll* have a glass of wine. (A pronunciation guide is provided from here on, to help you with the unfamiliar parts of each phrase.)

He'd like . . .	(Lui) vorrebbe un panino
	(*loo*-ee) vorreb-beh oon pan*ee*no
She'd like . . .	(Lei) vorrebbe un panino
	(lay) vorreb-beh oon pan*ee*no
Where can he get . . . ?	Dove può trovare (lui) una tazza di tè?
	dov-eh poo-*o* trovar-eh (*loo*-ee) oona *tat*-tza dee teh
Where can she get . . . ?	Dove può trovare (lei) una tazza di tè?
	dov-eh poo-*o* trovar-eh (lay) oona *tat*-tza dee teh
He'll have . . .	(Lui) prende un bicchiere di vino
	(*loo*-ee) prendeh oon beec-kee-*air*eh dee v*ee*no
She'll have . . .	(Lei) prende un bicchiere di vino
	(lay) prendeh oon beec-kee-*air*eh dee v*ee*no
He needs . . .	(Lui) avrebbe bisogno di una ricevuta
	(*loo*-ee) avreb-beh beez*on*-yo dee oona reechev*oo*ta
She needs . . .	(Lei) avrebbe bisogno di una ricevuta
	(lay) avreb-beh beez*on*-yo dee oona reechev*oo*ta

You can also help a couple or a group if they are having difficulties. The Italian word for *they* is **loro**, but it is usually left out altogether. Look at the verb ending:

They'd like ...	**(Loro) vorrebbero del formaggio** (loro) vorreb-bero del form*a*d-jo
Where can they get ... ?	**Dove possono trovare dell'aspirina?** d*o*v-eh p*o*s-sonno trov*a*r-eh del-laspir*ee*na
They'll have ..	**Prendono del vino** pr*e*ndono del v*ee*no
They need ...	**Avrebbero bisogno di acqua** avr*e*b-bero beez*o*n-yo dee *a*cqua

What about the two of you? No problem. The word for *we* is **noi** (noy), but it is only really important to change the verb ending:

We'd like ...	**Vorremmo del vino** vorr*e*m-mo del v*ee*no
Where can we get ... ?	**Dove possiamo trovare dell'acqua?** d*o*v-eh pos-see-*a*m-o trov*a*r-eh del-l*a*cqua
We'll have ...	**Prendiamo della birra** prendee-*a*m-o della b*e*erra
We need ...	**Avremmo bisogno di aspirina** avr*e*m-mo beez*o*n-yo dee aspir*ee*na

Try writing out your own checklists for these four useful phrase-starters, like this:

Vorrei ...	**Vorremmo ...**
Vorrebbe (lui) ...	**Vorrebbero ...**
Vorrebbe (lei) ...	
Dove posso trovare ... ?	
Dove può trovare (lui) ... ?	**Dove ... trovare ... ? (noi)**
Dove può trovare (lei) ... ?	**Dove ... trovare ... ? (loro)**

You will find more practice on the next page.

MORE PRACTICE

Here are some more Italian names of things. See how many different
sentences you can make up, using the various points of information
given earlier in this section.

		singular	plural
1	ashtray	portacenere (*m*)	portaceneri
2	bag	borsa (*f*)	borse
3	car	macchina (*f*)	macchine
4	cigarette	sigaretta (*f*)	sigarette
5	corkscrew	cavatappi (*m*)	cavatappi
6	deckchair	sedia a sdraio (*f*)	sedie a sdraio
7	garage (repairs)	autoriparazioni (*f*)	autoriparazioni
8	grapes	uva (*f*)	(*no plural*)
9	ice-cream	gelato (*m*)	gelati
10	melon	melone (*m*)	meloni
11	passport	passaporto (*m*)	passaporti
12	rag (dishcloth)	straccio (*m*)	stracci
	NB this word takes 'lo' and 'uno'		
13	salad (lettuce)	insalata (*f*)	insalate
14	shoe	scarpa (*f*)	scarpe
15	stamp	francobollo (*m*)	francobolli
16	station	stazione (*f*)	stazioni
17	sunglasses		occhiali da sole (*m*)
18	telephone	telefono (*m*)	telefoni
19	telephone token	gettone (*m*)	gettoni
20	ticket	biglietto (*m*)	biglietti

Index

Notes

Notes

Notes

Notes